Editing by Swami Anand Burt

Typesetting by Ma Prem Arya

Design by Ma Dhyan Amiyo

Paintings by Ma Anand Meera (Kasué Hashimoto), B.F.A.
(Musashino Art University, Tokyo)

Photography by Swami Svatantra Sarjano

Production by Swami Prem Visarjan; Swami Prem Prabodh

Printing by Mohndruck, Gütersloh, West Germany

Published by The Rebel Publishing House GmbH
Cologne, West Germany

Copyright © Neo-Sannyas International

First Edition

All rights reserved

No part of this book may be reproduced or transmitted in any form or by any means electronic or mechanical including photocopying or recording or by any information storage and retrieval system without permission in writing from the publisher.

ISBN 3-89338-063-9

In loving gratitude to Osho Rajneesh
Rajneesh Foundation Australia

DŌGEN
THE ZEN MASTER
A SEARCH AND A FULFILLMENT

Talks given to the
Rajneesh International University of Mysticism
in Gautama the Buddha Auditorium
Poona, India
from July 25 – August 1, 1988

OSHO RAJNEESH

DŌGEN
THE ZEN MASTER
A SEARCH AND A FULFILLMENT

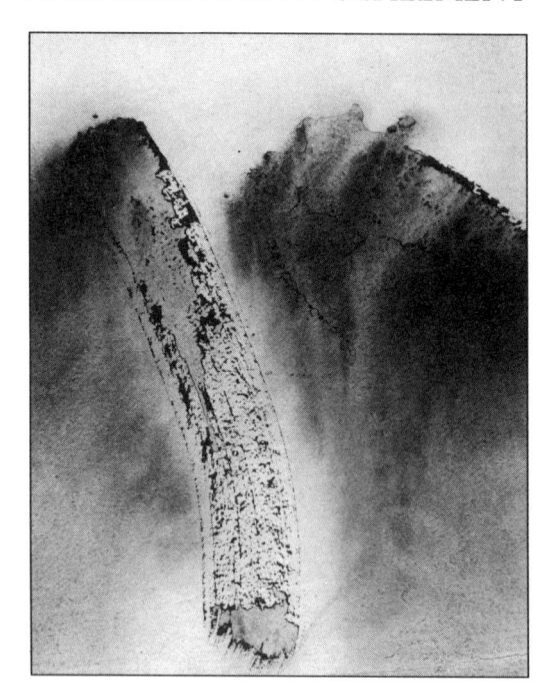

Dedicated to the Full Moons

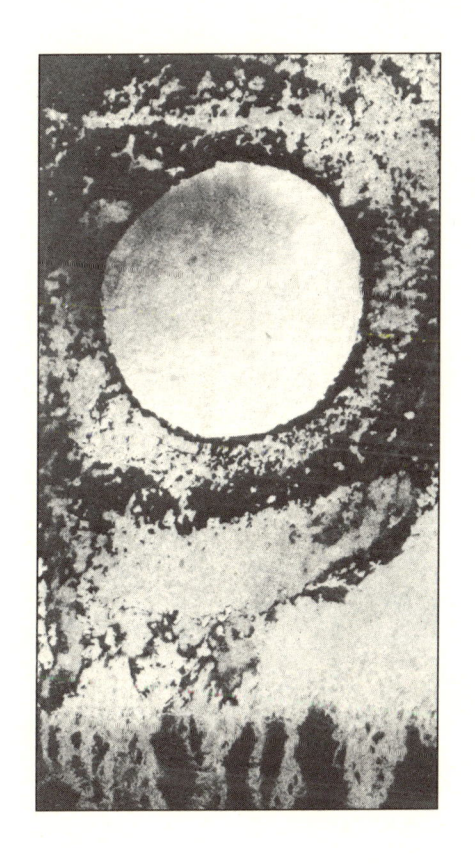

Introduction	VIII
Note to the reader	X
To study the way… To forget the self…	1
Firewood and ash	21
The mountainless ocean	41

TABLE OF CONTENTS

65	Dive a little deep
91	The moon never breaks the water
111	The sky is not scratched by the cloud
137	Live one day as a buddha
161	Secretly, a jewel in his robe

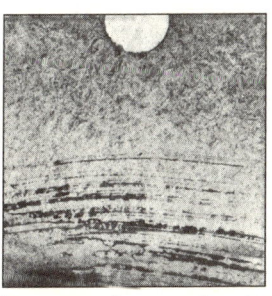

There is only one ultimate experience, but there are thousands of expressions of it – there is only one moon, but thousands of reflections of it: in every dewdrop sliding across a lotus leaf, in every pool. Ripples and waves may break the reflection, but when stillness returns the reflection is seen again.

Osho Rajneesh uses this beautiful and evocative metaphor to help explain enlightenment the Zen way, in this series of discourses about the unique Zen master Dōgen. Dōgen was a child of genius, never satisfied with borrowed knowledge. His journey from child to man, from scholar to enlightened master is traced through these sutras by Osho Rajneesh.

In his search for the truth, Dōgen soared high and eventually reached the ultimate peaks that have no beginning and no end. Like a breeze disappearing in the

INTRODUCTION

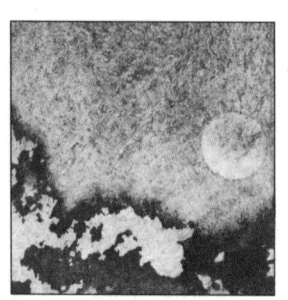

air, or a dew-drop merging with the ocean, Dōgen merged with the formless, with the changeless.

Illuminating this tremendous journey with stories and incredibly beautiful haikus, Osho Rajneesh reminds us that the ultimate experience can also be ours. Neither age nor birth, nor country nor race is of any importance – only awareness matters. The ultimate experience is so subtle that we have to be utterly silent to catch it. No special discipline is needed, no special situation, just the silence of being settled at the very center of our being.

We are part of a tremendous mystery, and must catch hold of it today. Tomorrow may be too late.

Ma Deva Prashanta

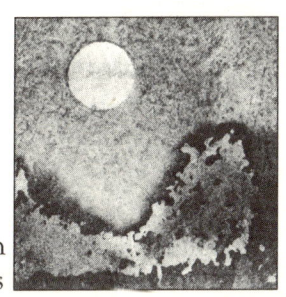

The end of each discourse in this series follows a certain format which might be puzzling to the reader who has not been present at the event itself.

First is the time of Sardar Gurudayal Singh. "Sardarji" is a longtime disciple whose hearty and infectious laughter has resulted in the joke-telling time being named in his honor.

The jokes are followed by a meditation consisting of four parts. Each stage of the meditation is preceded by a signal from Osho to the drummer, Nivedano. This drumbeat is represented in the text as follows:

NOTE TO THE READER

The first stage of the meditation is gibberish, which Osho has described as "cleansing your mind of all kinds of dust...speaking any language that you don't know... throwing all your craziness out." For several moments, the hall goes completely mad, as thousands of people shout, scream, babble nonsense and wave their arms about.

The gibberish is represented in the text as follows:

The second stage is a period of silent sitting, of focusing the consciousness on the center, the point of witnessing.

The third stage is "let-go" – each person falls effortlessly to the ground, allowing themselves to dissolve the boundaries that keep them separate.

A final drumbeat signals the assembly to return to a sitting position, as they are guided in making their experience of meditation more and more a part of everyday life. The participants are guided through each stage of the meditation by the words of the Master, and the entire text of each evening meditation is reproduced here.

TO STUDY THE WAY...
TO FORGET THE SELF...

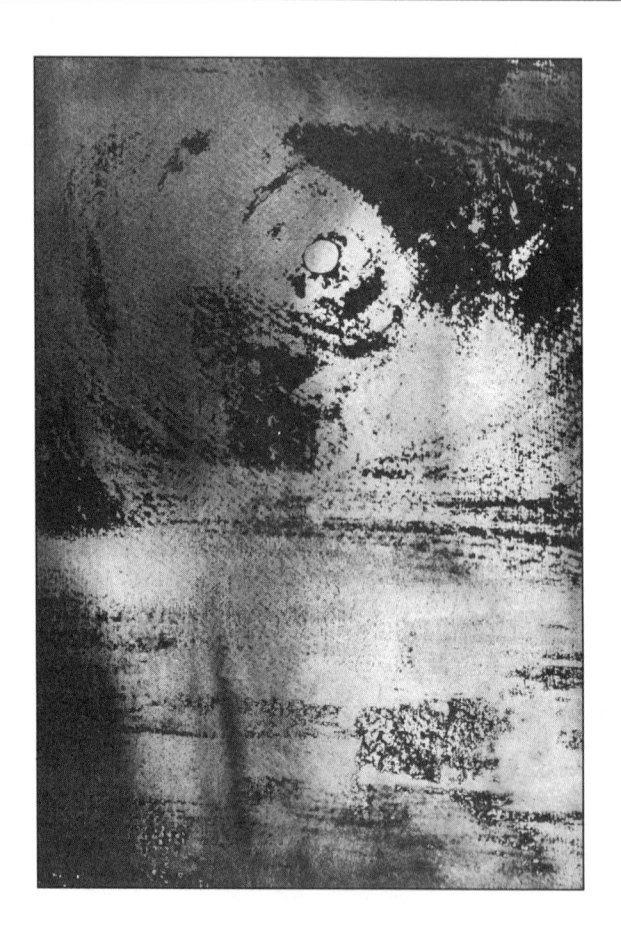

There are no doors inside.
It is an open space, an open sky.
But to know this open sky is to realize
the deathless principle of your existence.

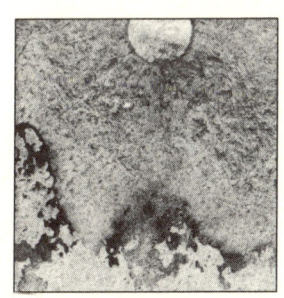

*Our Beloved Master,
Dōgen wrote:*
To study the Way is to study the self. To study the self is to forget the self. To forget the self is to be enlightened by all things. To be enlightened by all things is to remove the barriers between one's self and others. Then there is no trace of enlightenment, though enlightenment itself continues into one's daily life endlessly.

The first time we seek the Law, we are far away from the border of it. But soon after the Law has been correctly transmitted to us, we are enlightened persons.

Maneesha, this is the first day of a new series of talks, devoted to the full moons. The moon is an ancient symbol of transforming the hot rays of the sun into cool, peaceful, beautiful rays. It has nothing of its own. When you see the moon, you are seeing only a mirror which is reflecting the rays of the sun. Those reflected rays are just

TO STUDY THE WAY... TO FORGET THE SELF...

like the ones you can see when the sun is reflected in a river.

The moon is a mirror but not only a mirror, it is also a transforming agent. It changes the heat rays into cool, peaceful rays. That is the reason why the moon has become the most significant symbol in the East.

This series is dedicated to the full moons. In the series itself we are going to discuss one of the most unique masters, Dōgen.

Before I enter into the sutras, it will be good for you to know something about Dōgen. That background will help you to understand his very condensed sutras. Apparently they look contradictory. Without the background of Dōgen's life pattern they are like trees without roots, they cannot bring flowers. So first I will talk about Dōgen's life structure.

Dōgen was born into an aristocratic family in Kyoto, eight hundred years ago. His father was a high-ranking government minister and he himself was an uniquely intelligent child. It is said that he began to read Chinese poetry at the age of four—another Mozart.

Chinese is perhaps the most difficult language in the world, because it has no alphabet. It is pictorial and to read it means years of hard work to memorize those symbols. To the born Chinese it is not so difficult, because from the very birth it becomes ingrained into his mind, but anybody who is studying Chinese from the outside world... I have been told by friends that it takes ten years at least, if one works strenuously; thirty years if one works the way any ordinary student will work.

At the age of four, to understand Chinese—and not only Chinese, but Chinese poetry; that makes it even more difficult. Because to understand the prose of any language is simple, but the poetry has wings, it flies to faraway places. Prose is very marketplace, very earthly; it creeps on the earth. Poetry flies. What prose cannot say, poetry can manage to indicate. Prose is connected with your mind, poetry is more connected with your heart; it is more like love than like logic.

At the age of four, Dōgen's understanding of Chinese poetry immediately showed that he was not going to be an ordinary human being. From that very age his behavior was not that of a mediocre

child; he behaved like a buddha, so serene, so graceful, not interested in toys. All children are interested in toys, teddy-bears...who cares about poetry?

But, fortunately or unfortunately, his father died when he was only two years old and his mother died when he was seven. Dōgen used to say later on to his disciples, when he became a fully-fledged master in his own right, that everybody thought it was a misfortune: "What will happen to this beautiful, intelligent child?" But in his deepest heart he felt it was an opportunity; now there was no barrier.

Modern psychologists will perhaps understand it: you may be grown up—fifty, sixty, seventy—your father and mother may be dead...still they dominate you in a very psychological way. If you silently listen to the voices within you can work out that, "This voice comes from my father, or from my mother, or from my uncle, or from my teacher, or from the priest."

Dōgen used to say, "It was a great opportunity that both the people who could have distracted me, who loved me and I loved them...and that was the danger. They died at the right time. I am infinitely grateful to them just because they died at the right time without destroying me."

It is something very strange for a seven-year-old child to understand this. It has been discovered only now by the psychologists that man's greatest barriers are the father, the mother. If you want to be a totally free consciousness you have to drop, somewhere on the way, your teddy-bears, your toys, the teachings that have been forced upon you. They have all been of good intent, there is no question about it, but as it is said in an ancient proverb, "The path to hell is paved with good intentions."

Just good intentions are not enough; what is needed is a conscious intention, which is very rare. To find a father and mother with a conscious meditative energy is just hoping for the hopeless.

When his mother died Dōgen was translating the most significant Buddhist scripture, *Abhidharma*—"the essence of religion"—from Chinese into Japanese. He showed every sign of a tremendous future. And at the age of seven, when his father and mother had both died, the first thing he did—which is unbelievable—was to become a

sannyasin. Even the neighbors, relatives, could not believe it. And Dōgen said, "I will not miss this opportunity. Perhaps if my father and mother were alive, I might not have left the world in search of truth." He became a sannyasin and started searching for the master.

There are two kinds of seekers who become interested in truth. One starts looking for scriptures: he may become a great intellectual, he may become a giant, but inside there will be darkness. All his light is borrowed, and a borrowed light is not going to help in the real crises of life.

I am reminded of a Christian priest who used to repeat in every sermon Christ's saying, "If somebody slaps you on one cheek, give him the other, too." Everybody liked his sermons, he was quoting such great statements. But in one place a man really stood up and slapped the priest on one of his cheeks. The priest was shocked, because he had just been quoting Jesus. But anyway, to save his face, he gave his other cheek. And that man must have been a real rebellious type; he slapped the other one, too. Now this was too much!

The priest jumped at the man and started beating him. And the man said, "What are you doing?"

He said, "The scripture stops with the second cheek. Now I am here and you are here: let us decide this."

Borrowed scriptures won't help in actual encounters. In life there are everyday realities to be faced. In death the ultimate reality has to be faced. And borrowed knowledge is not going to help at all.

The second type of seeker does not go towards the scriptures, but starts searching for a master. These are two different dimensions: one is looking for knowledge, the other is looking for a source which is still alive. One is looking for dead scriptures, the other is looking for a living scripture whose heart is still beating and dancing, in whose eyes you can still see the depth, in whose presence you can see your own potential.

This second type is authentically the seeker for truth. The first type is only a seeker for knowledge.

You can have tons of knowledge and still you will remain ignorant. The man who has found the master may have to drop all his knowledge so that he can become open and vulnerable to the

master's presence, so that he can dance with the master's heart. In this dance there happens a synchronicity, both the hearts slowly settle into the same rhythm. This rhythm is called the transmission. Nothing visible is given—no teaching, no doctrine—but invisibly two hearts have started dancing in the same tune. All that the master knows slowly goes on this invisible track and pours into the hearts of the disciples to the point of overflowing.

Dōgen shows his intelligence, certainly, that he never turned to the scriptures. While his mother was alive, he was translating *Abhidharma,* one of the most important Buddhist scriptures, from Chinese into Japanese. If his parents had lived, he might have become a great scholar. After his parents had died, he burned all that he had translated with that scripture, *Abhidharma.*

It is so unbelievable. A seven-year-old child had the great insight that, "Words won't quench my thirst. I have to go in search of a living source, of someone who has known not by words, but by actual experience; one who is existentially a buddha."

The search for the master is the search for the buddha.

At the age of thirteen Dōgen was formally initiated. It was not easy to be initiated, one had to prove one's capacity, potentiality, possibility. One had to prove that one will not betray on the path, that one will not waste the time of the master, that one will wait infinitely. So he had to wait until the age of thirteen, and then:

He was formally initiated into the monkhood on Mount Hiei, the center of Tendai Buddhist learning in Japan. For the next several years he studied the schools of Mahayana and Hinayana, versions of Buddhism, under the guidance of his teacher, Abbot Kōen.

By the time he was fourteen Dōgen had become troubled by a deep doubt concerning one aspect of the Buddhist teaching.

This is the sutra that made him troubled to the very core of his being.

If, as the sutras say, "all human beings are endowed with the buddha-nature," why is it that one must train oneself so strenuously to realize that buddha-nature, to attain enlightenment?

A very significant question. If everybody is a buddha, then to recognize it should be the simplest thing in the world. If you are

TO STUDY THE WAY... TO FORGET THE SELF...

potentially a buddha, then the barriers cannot be much; they cannot hinder you. Nothing can hinder you. A rose bush brings roses, a lotus seed brings the lotus. If every man is a seed buddha, then why so much discipline? He was only fourteen years of age, and just one year before he had been initiated, but this sutra disturbed him immensely.

It is obvious that if to be a buddha is our nature, then it should be the simplest thing...without any discipline, without any effort—just a natural phenomenon, as you breathe, as your heart beats, as your blood runs in the body. There is no need of all the nonsense that has been forced upon people to become buddhas, to achieve buddhahood.

At this point he left his teacher because the teacher could not answer him. The teacher was just a teacher. He could teach the sutras, but he could not answer. He could realize the great significance of the question. Either buddhahood is not everybody's nature ...it is some faraway mountaintop, that you have to travel through all kinds of hardships to reach. But if it is your very nature, then *this* very moment you can realize it—there is no need even to wait for a single moment. But the teacher could not say that, because he himself had not realized buddhahood. He had been teaching Buddhist scriptures, and not a single student had ever said, "This sutra is contradictory."

In search of someone who could help rid him of his doubt,
Dōgen found himself with another teacher, Myōzen.

Teachers are many. Just to graduate into a certain branch of knowledge is not anything unique or special. But to find a master is really arduous, in that they both speak the same language—the teacher, the master. And sometimes it may be that the teacher speaks more clearly, because he is not worried about his own experience. The master speaks hesitantly, because he knows whatever he is saying is not perfectly appropriate, does not express the experience itself...that it is a little way off.

The teacher can speak with full confidence because he knows nothing. The master either remains silent or, if he speaks, he speaks with a great responsibility, knowing that he is going to make statements which appear to be contradictory, but which are not.

But every teacher wants to be known as a master. For the seeker

this creates a problem. Myōzen also proclaimed himself a master, but time proved that he was not a master.

In spite of long years of training under Myōzen, Dōgen still felt unfulfilled. At the age of twenty-three he decided to make the journey to China with Myōzen, in order to study Zen Buddhism further. Leaving the ship, Dōgen found his way to T'ien-t'ung monastery, where he trained under Master Wu-Chi. Still unsatisfied, for the next several months he visited numerous monasteries. Just as he was about to give up his search and return to Japan, he happened to hear that the former abbot of T'ien-t'ung had died, and that his successor, Ju-ching, was said to be one of China's finest Zen masters.

He changed his plan to go back to Japan and went again to the same monastery where he had been.

The old master, who was just a teacher, was dead, and he had been succeeded by Ju-ching—a man who had soared high and touched the peaks of consciousness, who had dived deep and touched the depths of his being, who had moved vertically upwards and downwards, who had traveled through all his conscious territory. This man Ju-ching proved to be a man who answered doubts, settled them, because Dōgen was still carrying the same question: that if buddhahood is your nature, then why is any discipline needed?

It was Ju-ching who said, "No discipline is needed. No discipline, nowhere to go, no way to be traveled...just *be*, silent, settled, at the very center of your being, and you are a buddha. You are missing it because you are looking and trying everywhere else except within you. You will never find your buddhahood by changing this monastery for another monastery, this master for another master. Go in!"

Ju-ching is known as one of the finest masters, a very fine sword that cuts things immediately. His presence, his fragrance, his grace... Dōgen remained with him, never asking a question, just drinking the very presence of the master, the very atmosphere, the very climate getting drowned.

And a moment always comes... An ancient Tibetan proverb says, "If the disciple is ready, the master appears." The whole question is of the disciple being ready. But the disciple can be ready only if he

TO STUDY THE WAY... TO FORGET THE SELF...

comes across a man of consciousness—not a man only of words, but a man of the experience—who has been to the highest peaks, to the lowest depths. And just being close to him one can feel the vibe, the coolness.

He radiates the truth; and if you are ready, suddenly something clicks. All doubts disappear, you know you have found the master. Now there is nothing to be asked. Whatever is needed, the master will give it. In fact, it is only because of the poverty of language that we say, "The master will give it." The truth is, when you are ready it simply showers on you—the master cannot even prevent it. The master is already radiating, just the doors of your being are closed. So those vibrations, and they are simply vibrations, return back. If the doors are open, nothing is said and everything is understood.

When Dōgen became a master in his own right, when Ju-ching declared to him, "Now, no more play the role of being a disciple," at that moment he hit Dōgen and said, "You have come to understand; now be compassionate on the blind humanity. Now don't go on sitting by my side. You are a buddha. Just because you were wandering here and there, you could not understand. Then sitting by my side, silently...I have not given you anything. You have simply become centered, and in this centering is the inner revolution."

Dōgen wrote:
To study the Way is to study the self. Now these are tremendously valuable statements. He is saying, "Don't ask about the way—there is no way." *To study the Way is to study the self.* The way leads away, and the further you go in search, the more you are lost. Drop all going and remain at home, just doing nothing. As Bashō has said:
Ancient pond.
A frog jumps,
and great silence.
And Bashō was just sitting there, so he wrote a small poem, sitting silently, doing nothing:

A frog jumps in the ancient pond.
A little sound and then great silence.

We are little sounds in a great silence. Between us and the universe there is not much more difference than between a sound and silence.

In every temple in the East we have used different kinds of bells. Even today they are used without any understanding. The reason is to give you a message—you ring the bell, a sound is created from nowhere. It echoes in the empty temple, it re-echoes, and every echo becomes more silent, more silent, and finally it disappears. Our existence is nothing but a sound in an immense ocean of silence.

To study the Way is to study the self.

Don't bother about the way, just study yourself.

To study the self is to forget the self.

Who is going to study the self? The one who is going to study the self has already dropped the self. The one who is studying the self is the witness—your real self.

To study the self is to forget the self. To forget the self is to be
enlightened by all things.

Then it does not matter in what situation you are—any situation will make you enlightened. People have become enlightened in every kind of situation you can imagine. The question is, if the self is dropped—then you may be chopping wood or carrying water from the well, it does not matter. The moment there is no self—only a witnessing, a silent watchfulness—you are enlightened by all things.

To be enlightened by all things is to remove the barriers
between one's self and others.

To be enlightened simply means: neither I exist nor you exist. What exists is something transcendental to I and thou, something more, something bigger and higher.

Then there is no trace of enlightenment.... In such a small passage he has condensed so much. Each sentence could have become a scripture.

Then there is no trace of enlightenment, though enlightenment
itself continues into one's daily life endlessly.

Once you have become enlightened, it is not that every day you have to remember that you are enlightened; that every morning, shaving before the mirror, you have to remember that you are enlightened; or going to the market, you have to remember not to behave against

TO STUDY THE WAY... TO FORGET THE SELF...

enlightenment. Once you have become enlightened your every act is automatically of awareness, of consciousness. Soon you forget all about enlightenment because it has become your very body, your very bones, your very blood, your marrow—it has become your very being. Now there is no need to remember it.

There have been masters who have forgotten completely that they are enlightened because there is no need to remember it. Their masters have hit them on their heads. The Zen stick came into existence for very certain purposes. One of the purposes was that somebody who has become enlightened and is still sitting silently has to be hit to be made aware, "Now go away! Get on! Pick up your rented bicycle! What are you doing here?"

Enlightenment does not happen twice—once is enough. The master hits as a reward, to remind you, "Now there is no need to be near me."

There are beautiful stories...

Mahakashyapa became enlightened, and he would not even come near Buddha. He used to sit far away, under a tree; for years he had been meditating there. He became enlightened...now he was afraid to come close to Buddha because he would recognize. Buddha himself had to walk towards Mahakashyapa and say, "Mahakashyapa, don't try to deceive me. Now there is no need to sit under this tree. Get on and move! There are millions of people who are still groping in darkness, and you are sitting here enlightened. Take this fire of your enlightenment and make as many people aflame as possible."

Mahakashyapa had tears in his eyes. He said, "I have been hiding, who told you? I know that now this has happened a difficulty...I am enlightened, and I cannot go near to you. I want to touch your feet, but I touch your feet, make the gesture of touching your feet, just from far away under the tree. Because I know, once one is enlightened he will be sent away."

Another disciple of Gautam Buddha, Sariputta, made it a condition. When he took initiation he was already a very famous scholar of his time.

He made it a condition, "If by chance I become enlightened, please don't send me away. I want to remain always by your side. If

DŌGEN

enlightenment means that I will have to go away, I will not become enlightened, so it is up to you."

Buddha said, "Don't be worried. First become enlightened, then we will see."

He said, "No, I want it as a promise. Enlightenment is certain by your side. And if you don't give me a promise, you will be the barrier to my enlightenment."

Buddha said, "You are putting me into difficulty. If everybody starts saying, 'Don't send us away,' how I am going to manage?"—already ten thousand sannyasins were moving with him from one village to another village.

He said, "Sariputta, you are such a great scholar, you should understand. Because enlightenment is not only enlightenment, it is also a great responsibility. You have come to realize the ultimate peace, the joy, the blissfulness." Now it is your responsibility to share it, go as far away as possible. Now there is no point in sitting by the side of the master.

Then there is no trace of enlightenment, though enlightenment itself continues into one's daily life endlessly.
The first time we seek the Law—by law is meant the ultimate law of existence—*we are far away from the border of it. But soon after the Law has been correctly transmitted to us...*

I have explained to you what transmission is: it is not through words, it is through the presence. It is through being close, in trust, in love, that something jumps from the master's inner being and makes you aflame. It is a quantum leap of consciousness. It is almost like two candles: one is lit, another is unlit. If you bring both the candles closer, there will come a moment when the flame of the lit candle will take a jump—you can see the jump—and the unlit candle also becomes lit. And the lit candle does not lose anything. The unlit candle was carrying the possibility, the potentiality; it just needed an opportunity.

The master is the opportunity.
The first time we seek the Law we are far away from the border of it. But soon after the Law has been correctly transmitted to us, we are enlightened persons.

Everybody is a buddha, either awake or asleep. Only this small distinction exists; otherwise there is no lower or higher. There is nothing wrong in being a sleeping buddha—it is your choice. A little more sleep is not going to harm anybody—just don't snore, because that will create a disturbance in other people's sleep.

A Catholic priest was in great difficulty. An old man, the richest man of his congregation, used to sit in front of him, and he used to come with his small grandchild. And the old man, as the sermon would start, would start snoring. It was such a disturbance to the priest, but the man was rich and he was donating so much to the church that he could not be interfered with. But somehow it had to be stopped; otherwise sooner or later everybody would be sleeping, snoring, and he would be preaching to them. This disease had to be stopped.

He tried to find a way. He pulled the little child aside when they were leaving and asked him, "Can you do something, for God's sake?"

He said, "I never do anything without money. I don't know God or God's sake—just money." A real businessman's son.

The Catholic priest said, "Okay. I will give you a quarter dollar if you keep the old man awake. Whenever he snores wake him up—just hit him with your knee."

He said, "In advance, because I don't do anything without the money in advance. And if the old man comes to know, there is going to be trouble. So better give me the advance first, I am taking a risky job." The priest had to give him a quarter dollar.

The next Sunday morning, when the old man started snoring, the little boy hit him again and again to wake him up. The old man said, "What has happened to you? You used to sit silently. You have been coming with me always."

He said, "It is a business matter."

The old man said, "What do you mean?"

He said, "I am getting a quarter dollar to keep you awake."

The old man said, "That's simple—I will give you half a dollar to let me sleep."

He said, "Okay—in advance."

The old man gave him half a dollar and the boy stopped waking him up. The preacher made many signs to the boy, "Just do something!" But the boy closed his eyes, as if he was in great meditation.

After the church, the priest caught hold of the boy saying, "You are very cunning. You took the money in advance, and for half of the sermon you were doing perfectly well. Then why did you start behaving in such a way—as if you were meditating? For years I have been seeing you; you have never closed your eyes."

He said, "You don't understand: business is business."

The priest said, "What do you mean?"

He said, "The old man has given me half a dollar. Naturally, I had to stop. Now, if you are ready for one dollar next Sunday... But it is always a risk; the old man may give me two dollars."

The priest thought, "This is a difficult thing for a poor priest. The rise of the price will go on, because that old man is rich, he can give anything."

He thought, "It is better to talk to the old man." He said to him, "I don't object to your sleep because sleep is not—according to the holy scriptures—a sin. You can sleep. But snoring...that too is not sin according to any holy scripture, but it interferes with other sleepers. And to interfere in somebody else's life is certainly immoral. There are many others who are sleeping, I know. But who comes to the church? People who are utterly tired come to the church to have at least a good morning sleep. You are disturbing them. And this boy is going to prove a great businessman. He has already managed...he asked for payment in advance."

The old man said, "There is no point in getting into competition because, whatever price has to be given, I will give. But for God's sake let me sleep—and I am going to snore. It is my birthright."

This much is the difference between your essential buddhahood and your snoring buddhahood. Just give a good shake...

You will be surprised to know that there used to be two groups of Christians: one was called "Quakers" and the other was called "Shakers." In their church the Quakers quake just to keep themselves awake, and the Shakers shake just to keep themselves awake. I

TO STUDY THE WAY... TO FORGET THE SELF...

think those two groups, which have almost disappeared, represent the most essential part of any religion. Christianity is poorer because of the decline of those two groups.

It is perfectly right if you can help to wake up your buddha by shaking. What is wrong with it? What are you doing in the Dynamic Meditation? It is just a mix of shaking and quaking.

Soon you will be entering into our every evening's meditation and you will see that nobody ever has disturbed the sleep so much—not only their own, but for miles around nobody can sleep. We are determined to make everybody a buddha.

Maneesha has asked:

Our Beloved Master,
To forget the self—to remember the self:
are these two different paths or, in some way, are they the same?

They are the same, just different expressions. One can say something positively; one can say the same thing negatively. But they both are saying the same. Remembering the self, the self will disappear. The more you remember, the more you will find it is not there.

Forgetting the self is the same. You are beyond yourself; don't cling to your "I", to your ego, to your personality. Just drop clinging to this cage, move out of the cage, and the whole sky is yours. Open your wings and fly across the sun like an eagle.

In the inner sky, in the inner world, freedom is the highest value —everything else is secondary, even blissfulness, ecstasy. There are thousands of flowers, uncountable, but they all become possible in the climate of freedom.

Before we enter into our meditation, I have to wake up all those who have fallen asleep by now.

Dodoski and Nerdski are sitting in the local jail charged with disturbing the peace and being drunk and disorderly.

That afternoon, Sergeant Crapski takes the boys to a big field to

DŌGEN

do some civic duty work while they serve their time.

"Okay," says the cop. "Like I told you guys before, you can start digging that trench."

The officer gives a shovel to each of them, points vaguely out at the ten-acre lot, and then walks away.

Nerdski looks around for a while, then turning to Dodoski says, "Dig *what* trench? I don't see any trench."

...Do any of you see?

Nerdski is out of work so he goes up to Beverly Hills. He goes around from mansion to mansion, offering to do odd jobs. Finally, at one huge estate, Nerdski knocks on the door.

"Got any work you need doing?" he asks.

"What can you do?" asks the owner.

"I'm a really good painter," replies Nerdski.

"Great!" says the man, handing him a can of green paint. "You can go round the back and paint the porch green. It is pretty big, so it will probably take you all day."

But two hours later, Nerdski knocks again at the front door. "I've finished that porch," he tells the owner.

"Wow," says the man. "That was really fast."

"No problem for me," says Nerdski proudly. "I'm a professional."

"Okay," says the man. "Here is your money."

"Thanks," says Nerdski and turns to leave. "By the way," he adds. "That's not a porch, it's a Ferrari!"

Kowalski is on holiday in a small town in the Italian Alps. After a few lonely nights he begins to feel the need for a woman. So he asks the local bartender how to find the ladies of the town.

"We gotta no prostitutes," replies the bartender. "The priest-a would never allow it. But the thing-a you want is-a kept out of sight,"

"What have I got to do?" asks Kowalski.

The bartender explains that up in the mountains there are caves. "Go there after dark-a," he says. "And shout-a 'Yoo-Hoo!' into the

cave. And if the lady calls back, 'Yoo-Hoo,' you work out-a the price. If she is busy, you get no answer."

So that night, Kowalski "Yoo-Hoo's" his way from cave to cave, but with no luck. Finally he decides to go back to town to get drunk, but at the bottom of the mountain he finds a cave that he has not seen before.

"Yoo-Hoo, Yoo-Hoo!" he shouts.

"Yoo-Hoo, Yoo-Hoo!" comes back the clear reply.

So Kowalski rushes into the cave—and is knocked flat by a train!

Jimmy is lost in the desert with two friends, Billy and Sammy. They wander around for two days, almost dying of thirst, until they come to a nunnery.

They knock on the door and the Mother Superior answers.

"Water, water, please give us water!" they groan.

"Oh, no," says the nun. "We had a man in here before. If you want to come in here for water, you have to let us cut off your pricks."

The three guys run back out into the desert. But two days later they figure that they will die anyway, so what the hell. They go back to the nunnery and say that they accept the condition.

They are brought in and the head nun takes Billy into another room. There is a short scream and then the nun comes back for Sammy. She takes him into another room and there is another, longer drawn-out, scream. But when she comes back for Jimmy, he is terrified.

"Just a minute!" he cries. "How did you cut their pricks off?"

"Simple," says the nun. "We ask them what their profession is. The first guy is a butcher, so we cut it off with a knife. The second guy is a carpenter, so we sawed it off."

At this point, Jimmy starts laughing hysterically with tears rolling down his cheeks.

"What's so funny?" asks the nun.

"You're gonna have trouble with me," laughs Jimmy. "I work for Kwality Ice Cream!"

Now...everybody is awake.

DŌGEN

Nivedano...

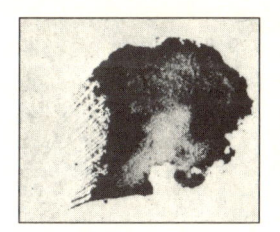

Nivedano...

Be silent...
close your eyes...
Feel as if you are frozen.
Enter in.
The deeper you can,
the more you will experience
your buddha-nature.
At the deepest point,
you are the ultimate reality—
immortal, eternal,
with all the blessings

that you can ever conceive of.
Don't miss the opportunity.
It is the simplest thing in the world
to go in...because it is your own home.
You need not even knock on the doors.
In fact there are no doors inside.
It is an open space, an open sky.
But to know this open sky
is to realize
the deathless principle of your existence.
Deeper, deeper, and deeper...
Drink this life juice to your heart's content.
And remember this peace, this silence,
this blissfulness.
Around the day,
whatever you are doing, don't forget it.
Like an undercurrent,
let it remain there. And slowly, slowly
it will change your whole life structure.

To make it more clear—sharply clear,
Nivedano...

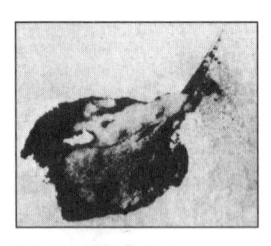

You relax...
let go...
as if you have died.
One day you will.
This is just a rehearsal.
Leave the body,
forget the mind...

and move as deep as you can,
like an arrow...fast,
hitting the very center.
This is the buddha.

Nivedano...

Come back.
But come back as buddhas,
knowing perfectly your eternal being.
Just sit down for a few seconds
to recall the memory
of the territory that you have traveled,
of the center that you have touched.
Let it become your breathing,
let it become your heartbeat.

To be a buddha is so simple,
you don't have to go anywhere.
You have to just stop going anywhere,
and just be within yourself.

Okay, Maneesha?
Yes, Beloved Master.

Can we celebrate the ten thousand buddhas?
Yes, Beloved Master.

FIREWOOD AND ASH

One full moon;
Stars numberless; the sky
dark green.

Our Beloved Master,
Dōgen continues:
When we look back at the shore from our boat, we mistakenly feel as if the shore were moving. But when we look at our boat with care, we find that it is our boat that is actually moving. Similarly, when we see all things with the deluded idea that our body and mind are separate from each other, we mistakenly think innate mind and nature are eternal. But when we realize that our body and mind are inseparable, we see clearly that all things are not substantial.

Firewood, when burned, becomes ash; the ash never again reverts to being firewood. Still, we should not regard firewood as a before, and ash as an after. We must realize that firewood is in the position of firewood with or without before and after. Ash is in the position of ash with or without before and after.

We can no more come back to life after our death than firewood can become firewood again after having become ash. In Buddhism, therefore, it is said that life never becomes death; life is beyond the conception of

life. It says that death does not become life; death is beyond that of death. Life and death are both only one stage of time, just like winter and spring.

Likewise, we must not think that winter becomes spring, or say that spring becomes summer.

Maneesha, Dōgen is basically concerned about the idea of reincarnation. Christianity does not accept it, Mohammedanism does not accept it, nor does Judaism accept it; it is only accepted by the religions that have been born in India. They may differ on every aspect of life, but on one point they are absolutely in agreement. And it is not an agreement of one day—for thousands of years they have agreed on the idea of reincarnation.

In Christianity or Mohammedanism or Judaism your life span is very short, just between the cradle and the grave—maybe seventy years or eighty years. With death you are finished. But in the Eastern experience, with death you only change your form. You are not finished, you continue. Your continuity is eternal. You will take many forms...many experiences, many ways of being.

This whole universe is conceived of in the East as a teaching period. The trees are learning to be trees, the birds are learning to be birds. This whole universe is exactly a great university, an opportunity to learn one form and also to learn that behind the form is hidden your formless being.

Thousands of times you have lived in different forms, experiencing different ways. Certainly to be a tree is a totally different experience than to be a bird or to be a lion. But the essential life is one. Out of this experience of essential life, the theory of reincarnation arose. And if you go deeper into your interiority...you can move so deeply that you will start touching not only your birth, your nine months in the womb, but also the death of the previous form.

It is a tremendous experience to know that you have been here before, because that gives another dimension to your consciousness; if you have been here in the past, you will be here in the future. The past and future both are in balance—the present moment is just the balancing moment. And if you can dig deep into the present

moment, you can experience not only your past lives; there is a possibility—if your effort is really total—that you may start having glimpses of your future possibilities.

Gautam Buddha is reported to have said that we never begin our journey—it is eternal. You cannot reach to the point, exploring within yourself, where you started the journey. That bus stop you cannot find. You have always been moving, traveling. So the beginning cannot be found, it is not there. But the end can be found.

You will be surprised to think about it—that the ordinary death is not a death because the consciousness moves into another form. A bird becomes a tree, a tree becomes an animal, an animal becomes a human being. But if your experience of all your past lives suddenly flashes you to the idea that you are eternal, that very moment you are disidentified with the body-mind structure. And this disidentification is the real death. Now you will not take another form, you will enter into the formless. It is called the great death.

But to have a great death you need to have a great life. Ordinary living is so lukewarm that ordinary death cannot change much; it can only change the outer garb, the paper bag in which you have been living. To burst forth out of all form—a tremendous awareness, intensity, totality...you pull all of yourself to a single point—and suddenly all forms disappear. Just like a breeze, invisible, you enter into the formless. This has to be remembered before I talk about Dogen, because that is exactly the background of what he is trying to say in the Zen way.

Dōgen continues:
When we look back at the shore from our boat, we mistakenly feel as if the shore were moving. But when we look at our boat with care, we find that it is our boat that is actually moving.

Now very few people have the experience of boats. Dōgen was talking to people who were traveling in boats continuously, because Japan is not one island; it is many islands together, and people are continuously moving in boats from one island to another.

But in your experience you may have...sitting in a train, suddenly you see that another train which was sitting on the side track has

started moving. But your experience is so clear that *you* are moving. Then you look to the other side—the station is still there. Then certainly, the other train is moving. But the station is gone, then the movement of that train was an illusion; your train is moving. Movement is relative, just as in geometry two parallel lines never meet.

Albert Einstein, the man who introduced the idea of relativity into the world of science, says that if two rockets are moving in the sky at the same speed, none of the passengers in either of the rockets will feel that there is any movement. Because to experience movement you need something stationary by the side; it is a relative experience. Both the rockets are moving in a silent, open sky at the same speed; naturally, you see there is no movement in the other rocket. And how can there be movement in your rocket? If there were, you would have passed the other rocket. None of the passengers in either of the rockets will even dream about movement, because there is nothing stable around; on both the sides, just pure sky. They can live in the illusion as long as they go on moving at the same speed.

According to Albert Einstein, a very strange conclusion...of course, it has not yet been tested, but it seems possible. If the passengers of both the rockets don't feel any movement, they will become very still and very silent. Not only in their minds, but even in their body cells the silence of no-movement will penetrate. It will be so enormous, so overwhelming, that when they return—you will be surprised—all their friends, their old colleagues, will have grown ten years older and they will not have aged at all. Those ten years they have missed. They have not moved a single inch, either in their body or in their mind, because movement has stopped being their experience.

Einstein was absolutely certain—and I agree with him. It seems absurd that a traveler will come back and find that his own generation is finished and a new generation has taken over, because he has been long away, traveling in the sky. But when there is no movement around you, slowly, slowly that non-movement stops everything moving within you: the mind, the body—everything.

Even he was shocked when he proposed the theory. It will still

take a few years for us to be absolutely certain of what he was saying, because even to reach to the nearest star takes four years; and the return journey means eight years—and this is the nearest star. We don't have yet any vehicle to move—without continuous fuel stations on the way—for four years.

Secondly, the moment you are out of the grip of gravitation.... You don't feel gravitation because you are born in gravitation. Otherwise the earth is pulling you down so forcibly...most of your aging is because of the pull of the earth. The area of gravitation is two hundred miles around the earth. Once you are out of the gravitation area, there is nothing to pull you down; you simply remain the same. The same gravitation that is killing you also keeps you rooted, because without gravitation you will be simply gone—just saying good-bye to each other and moving into the eternal, never to meet again. It is so vast...and the speed will be such that you will be burned by the speed.

There are practical problems; that's why Albert Einstein could not persuade anybody to take the risk. The speed has to be exactly the speed of light—that is the ultimate speed. One hundred and eighty-six thousand miles per second—at that speed everything stops. You can go around the universe for thousands of years and you will come back to the earth the same, as young as you had left. But it is just theoretical and hypothetical; it is difficult, for the simple, pragmatic reason that at the speed of light no metal can remain unmelted. The heat is so much that the vehicle in which you are moving will melt down, burning you with it.

You look...almost three thousand stones fall every day on the earth, all over the earth. You think they are stars falling. Stars are very big, but these are just small stones which have been caught in the gravitational area of the earth, and the earth has pulled them. But the force of the pull is such that even the stones burn up. Most of these three thousand stones never reach to the earth; they are burned before reaching it. A few stones have reached the earth and they have become great sacred places. For example, the Kaaba—the holy place of the Mohammedans; the stone there is an asteroid, it is not of the earth. Just because people saw that big stone coming from

the sky...the primitive mind thought it must be from God. And it was coming, burning bright like a sun, so big that it reached to the earth. In many museums you will find those stones, which are called meteorites.

These stones burn up because of the speed. So if we make a vehicle we have to find something which will not burn up at the speed of light. Up to now, there is no indication that we can create a vehicle or any material that can move with the speed of light. And unless we move with the speed of light we cannot reach the nearest star. With that speed in mind, the nearest star is four light years away. It is such a long distance, and our small boats and our airplanes and our rockets are still, in terms of the future, just toys.

But consciousness needs no form to travel, hence it can move with the speed of light. That is the Eastern way of looking at things: you have been around on many planets in many different lives, not only on this earth. Scientists accept that there are at least five hundred planets with life, but there is no communication. All kinds of efforts are being made to have some kind of dialogue or to find some way to know exactly who is there. But that is a limitation of the body.

For a man of consciousness, for a man who is a buddha, there is no limitation. No gravitation prevents him, no heat can burn him. He can travel around in different forms, taking birth on different planets.

The idea of reincarnation is a very great challenge. It is not a question of arguing; it is a question of experiencing in yourself that which cannot be burned, that which remembers having been in other bodies. And if it can move from one body to another body, there is no difficulty for it to move from one planet to another planet. And ultimately it has to move from all forms and disperse itself into the universal being. That is *nirvana*.

Nirvana is one of the most beautiful words; I don't think there is any other word in any language which has so much significance and meaning. Ordinarily it simply means blowing out the flame. You have a candle, and the flame is dancing, and you blow it out. Can you answer where the flame has gone? It must have gone somewhere. Nirvana means: your life is just like a flame—when it becomes

difficult to live in one body, one form, it simply moves into another form. The other form is determined by its desires, its longings. Be very conscious about your desires and your longings because they are creating the seed of a new form already, without your knowing.

I have experienced, with many people, taking them back to their old forms. And I was surprised—because there is no mention of this fact in any Eastern scripture—that somebody who is a man, when he remembers, he remembers himself as a woman in his past life. If he goes deeper he again remembers himself as a man.

At first I was puzzled, because it is not mentioned anywhere. But then I could see the point that every woman is desiring to be a man. She thinks, "I am confined in the home, and the man is enjoying everything." And every man thinks, once in a while, "The beauty, the mystery of a woman..." So it is very natural that you are creating your other form already without doing it consciously. If you are man you will be born as woman. And this is a vicious circle, because when you die, you die unconsciously; when you are born you are born unconsciously. So you don't know from where you are coming, or what was the reason for your taking this form.

The whole foundation of meditation is to make you so alert that you can see the forming of seeds and desires and drop them. If you can die without a seed...

If you die in a half-hearted way, not totally, with something incomplete, with something you wanted to do and death has come in between—then you cannot expect to disappear into the universal. Then the flame will take another home, according to your desires, your reincarnations.

Meditation simply means to drop, slowly slowly, all your desires. And when death comes, celebrate it; celebrate it because everything is complete and you are ready. This readiness and completeness will give you the ultimate freedom of formlessness. That formlessness is nirvana.

All these buddhas, like Dōgen, are pointing towards that formlessness. First, he is talking about relativity:

When we look back at the shore from our boat, we mistakenly feel as if the shore were moving. But when we look at our boat with care, we

find that it is our boat that is actually moving. Similarly, when we see all things with the deluded idea that our body and mind are separate from each other, we mistakenly think innate mind and nature are eternal. But when we realize that our body and mind are inseparable, we see clearly that all things are not substantial.

The body has a substantiality. When someone dies all the elements of the body dissolve into their sources: water into water and air into air and earth into earth. Only one invisible bird, weightless.... There have been experiments where a man was weighed while he was alive, and weighed again after he has died. The weight does not differ; he is the same weight both times. To the objective mind, it means that nothing has moved out, because if there is a soul which moves out of the body, then certainly it would have weight. Experiments have even been done putting the dying man in a glass case, so that they can see if something moves out.... It will have to break the glass somewhere. But the glass remains intact as the man dies.

These things have supported the atheists, who say that there is no such thing as a soul. These conclusions are absolutely rational but stupid. There is no contradiction in being both stupid and rational. Of course the intellectual person will be more profoundly stupid than ordinary idiots; ordinary idiots are simple people. But there are extraordinary idiots, and because of their rationality they have turned almost the whole world's mind toward being materialistic.

Half of the world is communist, which does not believe that there is anything in the body; it is just a combination of materials. The remaining half of the world, which thinks it is spiritual, only thinks; it never experiments.

The experiment is not to be done in a scientific lab.

It has to be done within yourself.

That's what we are doing here—to find something immaterial, invisible to the eyes, untouchable by the hands, but still the very heart of our being, the very throb of our being. Once you have known it all fear of death disappears. And a new courage—so fresh like a morning rose, still with dewdrops shining on it in the sun—a new courage to rebel against all that is traditionally accepted, that may be rationally accepted but is not based on the actual experience of meditation...

Other than meditation, there is no way to decide whether you are just matter or there is something immaterial. Without that immaterial part you lose all your splendor. Only that immaterial part of your being gives you dignity; it makes you not only a man, but makes you capable of touching the highest peak of being a buddha.

Firewood, when burned, becomes ash; the ash never reverts to being firewood. Still, we should not regard firewood as a before, and ash as an after. We must realize that firewood is in the position of firewood with or without before and after. Ash is in the position of ash with or without before and after.

What Dōgen is trying to say is that when firewood disappears into a heap of ash you should not think that something in existence has changed—only the form has changed. The ash was present in the firewood, unmanifest. The fire has helped the ash to become manifest and visible.

These are ways of saying some things which are more difficult to say directly. But I can say them directly to you; this is not an assembly of kindergarten seekers. What you are, you have been the same before, whatever the form, and if you can discover yourself then it does not matter in what form you will move. And if you can penetrate your self to its very center—because your self has a circumference and a center.... If you remain at the circumference then you will move into another form—but if your arrow reaches to the very center you have graduated from forms. Now you are capable of being one with the universe; now you can sing with the birds, dance with the flowers, shine with the stars. From a small dewdrop, you have become the very ocean.

In America, which has produced very few men who are worth quoting, one man is certainly significant, but seems to be almost forgotten. He is William James. He introduced this beautiful word 'oceanic'. People have forgotten him and his word because very few people reach to that experience. But here everybody has to reach to the experience...from the dewdrop to the ocean. Unless you experience 'oceanic' yourself, spreading in all ten directions, in absolute freedom, you have not used the great opportunity of life.

Dōgen is saying, *We can no more come back to life after our death than firewood can become firewood again after having become ash. In Buddhism, therefore, it is said that life never becomes death; life is beyond the conception of life. It says that death does not become life; death is beyond that of death. Life and death are both only one stage of time, just like winter and spring. Likewise, we must not think that winter becomes spring, or say that spring becomes summer.*

Dōgen is saying that forms don't change into other forms. Winter remains winter, summer remains summer, but something inner moves on from one climate to another climate...which is beyond birth and beyond death, which is beyond life, which simply is. You can give it any shape, any form, but you cannot take away its isness. This isness is the greatest discovery of the East, the West has missed it completely.

A haiku by Hokushi runs:

> *The moon on the pine;*
> *I keep hanging it—taking it off*
> *and gazing each time.*

I have told you the moon is one of the great symbols in the mystery school of Zen...you will come across the moon many times from different aspects.

The moon on the pine;
I keep hanging it...

Just try to understand the poetry.

I keep hanging it—taking it off
and gazing each time.

Certainly you cannot hang the moon and take it off; but what you can do, you can open your eyes and you can close your eyes. When you close your eyes you have taken the moon away. When you open your eyes you bring the moon again. And gazing at it every time—it never fulfills the desire, the longing for beautitude.

Another haiku runs,

One full moon;
Stars numberless; the sky
dark green.

These are not ordinary poetries, these are expressions of deep meditation. Night, and particularly moonlit nights, have been found to be very supportive to meditation. Now even science suspects that the moon has a certain effect on the mind; because most of the people who go mad, go mad on a full moon night, hence the word 'lunatic'. It comes from *luna,* the moon. Another word is 'moonstruck'....

More people commit suicide on the full moon than at any other time and more people have become enlightened on the full moon than at any other time. Science has its own reasons.... The moon is really a part of the earth. Some four billion years ago a great chunk of the earth separated from the earth. All our great oceans are because of that chunk; deep valleys were left for rain to fill and they became the oceans.

The moon has one sixth the gravitation of the earth, because it is one sixth the size. That means that gazing at the moon, you slowly, slowly become more light, the gravitation is less on your being. That

is the scientist's explanation. And you can see the effect on the seas, because they are holding the place of the moon...where the moon used to be once. That's why on the full moon there are great tides. In the human body there is eighty percent water, ocean water with the same chemicals. Just as tides arise in the ocean, something arises in the human being. If he is on the right track perhaps he may become enlightened.

And if he is on the wrong track he can commit suicide or commit a murder or go mad...there are thousands of ways. But there is only one way that reaches to your ultimate sensitivity, the way of meditation, the way of closing all outgoing doors and being in.

And once in a while these Zen meditators have opened their eyes and they have seen the moon or a sunset or a lotus, and out of their meditation a certain expression has arisen. Only through meditation will you be able to understand it—it is not poetry, it is not written with the mind, it is a heartfelt feeling.

One full moon;
Stars numberless; the sky
dark green.

If you are in deep meditation and you see this dark sky with so many stars and one single moon, immediately your silence will become immensely deeper.

These haikus are not meaningful for those who have not experienced anything of meditation.

A haiku by Shiki:

> *Evening moon:*
> *plum blossoms start to fall*
> *upon the lute.*

These are pictures seen by a deeply meditative consciousness. They don't mean anything, they are not supposed to have any meaning, they are pictorial.

Once Picasso was asked.... A man was watching him painting continuously for hours; finally he said, "I cannot resist asking, because I have been watching you paint for hours, but I can't make

any sense out of what you are painting. What is it? What is the meaning of it?"

Picasso looked at the man and said, "I don't know. You can ask the picture yourself."

The man said, "Are you insane or something?"

Picasso said, "Perhaps, but nobody asks the rose, 'Why are you so beautiful? Why are you here in the first place?' Nobody asks a sunset, nobody asks a full moon, but everybody goes on harassing me, 'What is the meaning of your painting?' There is no meaning, it is a statement. I have enjoyed it tremendously, just the colors, flowing into each other, creating strange patterns."

Meaning is no more relevant in the world of beauty. And what to say about the world of meditation?—no meaning, only significance. That's why those who have experienced have remained silent, or have spoken only to indicate to you the path to be silent.

Maneesha has asked,

Our Beloved Master,
What is our investment in repressing our memory of previous deaths?
Is it not true to say that if we could recall our deaths we might lose our fear of death and thus be able to live a fearless life?

Maneesha, this is certainly one of our great investments in forgetting the past, the previous life. Because if you remember it, you will not be able to be so foolish as to repeat the same game again. You have done it so many times; you have fallen in love, you have fallen out of love, so many times...so many romances! Our great investment is that each time we go to see the same film we forget that we have seen it before. Otherwise you will not go to see the movie, only once is enough.

But in life you don't complete the work in one time, in one lifetime. Your real work remains postponed and you go on playing games which are simply childish. The great investment is that you should not remember your whole past, otherwise you will feel yourself to be so much an idiot that enjoying life will become impossible. Only suicide will seem to be the right thing to do. But suicide leads

nowhere, it simply enters your consciousness into another womb of a lower kind, because you could not manage to live on a higher level.

The investment also includes forgetting that you have ever died. It is always somebody else who dies, you never die. Obviously—you see every day, you hear every day that somebody has died; but you never hear that you have died. Except in this Buddha Hall where you hear every day, "Now die and don't hold anything back, die completely."

People from the outside will think, "This is a madhouse. People who are fully alive suddenly die and then don't wait much...as they are called back, immediately they are back, sitting like buddhas!"

We are making it clear through our meditations that this is how it has been happening, you have been dying many times and again coming back. Whether you come after nine months...an unnecessary wastage of time, of a woman's life...then growing up and again playing the same role which you have played before....

In the East the world is called *sansara*. Sansara means the great wheel of life and death. It goes on moving, the same wheel, and you are clinging to the wheel and you go on moving with the wheel from one death to another, from one life to another. The investment is that unless you learn the lesson, you cannot come out of this vicious circle of life and death. But you *can* come out. Every night we try; you jump a little...it is old habit; when you come back you just try to find out where the wheel is. Soon you have forgotten about the center which was beyond life and death—suddenly you remember, "Where is the canteen?"

One naturally feels hungry after such a strenuous experience of dying and coming back, becoming a buddha...knowing perfectly well that anybody may be a buddha, "But I am not; I have my wife, I have my children to look after. Just for a moment is okay, but twenty-four hours a buddha will not only be boring, it will be also a torture to others."

From my very childhood I was interested just to sit and not to do anything. I have never done any homework; my teachers were angry, "What do you go on doing at home?"

I said, "I simply sit and enjoy."

My family, and whoever would be passing by used to say, "What are you doing?"

I said, "There is no need to do anything—to be is enough!"

And they would look at me and say, "You are crazy! Do something, otherwise you will end up in being nothing."

And they were right, I have ended in being nothing. But I am immensely happy that I started very early to see that the greatest joy is inside, nobody can give it to me. I have never participated in any game, I have never bothered about any work the family needed. Slowly, slowly my family started taking for granted that I was no more—my being or not being made no difference.

I have enjoyed the faces of my family when they looked at me as if they were looking at an insane person; I still enjoy to remember it. Naturally if you are not doing something people think you are wasting your life. The reality is that when you are not doing anything, when you are just being, you are finding the path towards your ultimate destiny.

Before we die and become buddhas...one time more, because one never knows about tomorrow, so better become tonight....

Just a few small laughs, because Sardar Gurudayal Singh is waiting very silently. And Avirbhava....

When Gozo the gorilla dies his female companion, Gertie, gets very horny. After a few months she begins to get violent, as her need for sex increases. Finally the zookeepers decide to get a man to make love to her.

They go downtown and pick up José, a big Mexican, and offer him twenty dollars to do the job.

They put a muzzle on Gertie's mouth, tie her arms to the bars, and then let the Mexican into the cage. When Gertie sees that José has an erection, she goes wild. She rips her arms loose from the bars and begins crushing him in her embrace.

"Help!" shouts José. "For Christ's sake, help!"

"Don't worry," shouts the keeper. "We'll get the elephant gun and shoot her!"

"No! No!" cries José. "Don't shoot her! Just get her muzzle off—I want to kiss her!"

Dodoski has fallen on hard times, so he turns to crime. He kidnaps the six-year-old son of the richest man in Warsaw. Dodoski writes the ransom note, asks for half a million dollars, and signs his name.

But he has forgotten the rich man's address. So he gives the note to the boy, and tells him to take it to his dad.

The boy does, and when he comes back with the money, he is carrying a note from his father.

It reads: "Here, take the filthy money, you rat. It's guys like you that give us Polacks a bad name!"

After a wild Saturday night of partying, Swami Deva Coconut is hauled off to a Sunday morning Mass by his Catholic girlfriend, Beverly. Since he is totally ignorant of the various rituals involved, Beverly is constantly coaching him.

"Bless yourself," she whispers. "Now kneel down—sit down—stand up—sit down again—cross yourself..."—and so on.

Perspiring from all this activity, Coconut takes out a handkerchief from his pocket to wipe his face. Then he lays it on his lap to dry.

Seeing this, Beverly leans over and whispers, "Is your zipper open?"

"No," replies Coconut hastily, "should it be?"

Donald Dickstein walks into an optician's office, carrying a cardboard box. He hands it to the optician who opens it and exclaims, "Wow! That's the biggest turd I've ever seen!"

"Isn't it a beauty?" says Donald. "I did it myself."

The optician is very impressed and says, "It must be at least two feet long."

"Twenty-five and a half inches, to be exact," boasts Donald. "And three inches in diameter."

"Incredible," says the optician. "How much does it weigh?"

"Two and a half pounds," is the proud reply.

"That is simply amazing!" exclaims the optician, unable to take

his eyes off the magnificent specimen. "But why bring it to me? I'm an optician."

"Well, you see," says Donald, "I have this problem. Every time I do one of these monsters, my eyes water!"

Now, Nivedano, do a real good job because skinhead Niskriya is back....

Nivedano...

Nivedano...

Be silent...
Close your eyes...
No movement of the body.
Let your whole consciousness gather inwards.

Deeper and deeper...
You are entering into your buddhahood.
Without any fear go in, it is your own home.

Except knowing this,
all knowledge is useless.
Except experiencing this
you have wasted your very life
in mundane things.
This is the sacred moment,
drink it as deeply as possible.
Be soaked through and through.
Buddhahood is not an achievement,
it is only a discovery,
it is only going within your paper bag.
You are not your bones,
you are not your head,
you are not even your heart,
you are this beyondness, this silence.
Even if for a single moment you can experience it
your whole life will have a transformation.

To make it more clear, Nivedano...

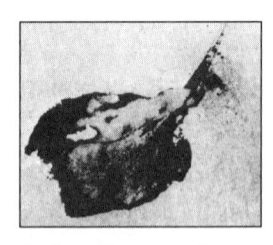

Relax..let go...die.
Die to the world, die to the body,
die to the mind,
so that only the eternal remains in you.
This formless eternal brings you a new birth.
You have entered as a human being,

you can come out of this womb of the beyond
as a buddha.

This bliss, this silence,
these roses blossoming within you,
they are your birthright. One can remain ignorant,
but one cannot be anything else than a buddha...
awakened, enlightened,
that is our very destiny.

Nivedano....

Come back
without forgetting the experience,
sit down for a while, just for a few moments
drop the doubt that you cannot be a buddha.
You are. In spite of yourself, you are.
If this becomes an undercurrent twenty-four hours,
waking or sleeping, your life will know
what this existence is all about.
You will know the freedom, the ultimate freedom which
you have been longing for
for many, many lives.
Don't miss it this time.

Okay, Mancesha?
Yes, Beloved Master.

Can we celebrate ten thousand buddhas together?
Yes, Beloved Master.

THE MOUNTAINLESS OCEAN

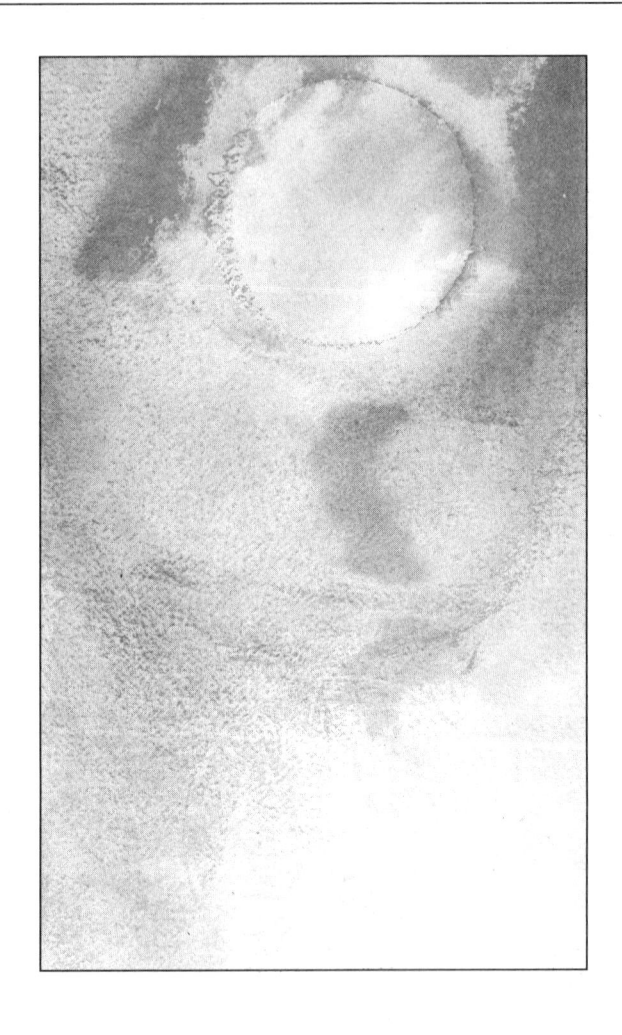

Skylark
sing all day,
and day not long enough.

*Our Beloved Master,
Dōgen continues:*
When we look around our boat on the mountainless ocean, we see nothing but the circular shape of the ocean. But this large ocean is not circular or square; its other shapes and movements are innumerable. To fish it is like a palace. To celestial beings it is like a necklace. Only as far as the eye can reach, does it temporarily appear circular.

This is also the case with all things. All things worldly and unworldly have various aspects, but we can see and realize them only through practical understanding....

However far fish sail in the water, there is no end to the water. However far birds fly in the sky, there is no end to the sky. But neither of them has ever left the water or the sky.

When their need is great, there is great activity; when their need is small, there is little activity. Thus they never fail to express their full ability in each thing, and exert their free activity in each place.

But as soon as a bird leaves the sky, it dies. This is also the case when

THE MOUNTAINLESS OCEAN

a fish leaves the water. We can realize that the water is life to the fish; that the sky is life to the bird; that the bird is life to the sky; the fish is life to the water; that life is a bird, or that life is the fish. About this there may be many other expressions.

In the human world there are practice and enlightenment, or long life and short life. This is also the real state of things. Nevertheless, if a bird or fish tries to go through the sky or the water after knowing it completely, it will find no way to go along or no place to attain.

Maneesha, Eastern mysticism has accepted layers of reality. Western science knows only one reality—that of matter. It is poor, it lacks variety. The Eastern mysticism, of which Zen is just the ultimate peak, accepts the reality of your inner self which you cannot see, cannot understand, but which you are. You can be awakened to it or you can remain asleep, it makes no difference to the inner quality of your being. That is your ultimate reality.

Then there is the body, which is only an appearance—an appearance in the sense that it is changing constantly. You see a beautiful woman or a beautiful man and they are already becoming old. The moment you rejoice in the beauty of a rose, the time for it to disappear back into the earth is not far away. This kind of reality has also its place in the Eastern vision. They call it appearance, moment to moment changing. There is a time to be born and there is a time to die. The seasons will come again, and the flowers will blossom again. It is the round trip of existence in which—except your being, your center—everything goes on changing. This changing world is a relative reality.

And then there are other realities—like dreams. You know they are not, but still you see them. Not only do you see them, they affect you. If you have a nightmare and you wake up, you will see your heart is beating harder, your breath is changed by the nightmare. You may be even perspiring out of fear. You cannot say that the nightmare is not there; otherwise from where has this perspiration come, and this changed heartbeat and breathing?

Eastern mysticism accepts this third layer of reality: the dream,

the horizon that you see all around, which exists nowhere...but you can see it from anywhere.

Before I explain Dōgen to you, let this be the introduction, because this is what he is trying to say: that everything passes and yet there is something that never passes; that everything is born and dies and yet there is something that is never born and never dies. And unless you get centered into that eternal source you will not find peace, you will not find serenity, you will not find blissfulness, you will not find contentment. You will not feel at home, at ease in the universe. You will remain just an accident, you will never become essential.

And the whole effort of Zen, or any meditative method, is to bring you closer to that which never changes, that which is always. It knows no time.... If there is no change, how can there be past, future, present? The world that knows past, future and present can only be relatively real—today it is there, tomorrow it is gone. The body you had believed in so much one day dies. The mind you had believed in so much does not follow you, it dies with the body. It has been a part of the body mechanism.

That which flies out of the body in death is an invisible bird flying into an invisible sky. But if you are aware you will be dancing, because for the first time you will have known what freedom is. It is not a political freedom or an economic freedom; it is a more fundamental, existential freedom. And anything that grows out of this freedom is beautiful, graceful. Your eyes are the same, but their vision has changed. Your love is there but it is no more lust, it is no more possessiveness. It transforms itself into compassion. You still share your joy in your songs, in your dances, in your poetry, in your music —but just for their sheer joy.

It has been a centuries-long debate: What is art for? There have been pragmatic utilitarians who say that art should serve some purpose, otherwise it is useless. But these people don't know art. Art can only be for its own sake. It is the sheer joy of a solitary cuckoo, of the bamboos standing in silence, of a bird flying into the sky. Just the very flight, the very feel of freedom, is enough unto itself. It need not serve anything else.

But that is possible only if you have known your fundamental existence. You are acquainted with the mind, which is borrowed, which is nurtured, educated. You are acquainted with your body very superficially. You don't know how it functions, although it is your body. You don't know how it turns food into blood, how it distributes oxygen to different parts of the body.

The body has its own wisdom. Nature has not left it to you to remember breathing, because you can forget. You are so sleepy, nature cannot take the risk. If you had to remember breathing, I don't think you would have been here. You would have been forgotten long before.

But whether you remember or not, whether you are awake or asleep, the breathing continues on its own, the heart goes on working on its own, the stomach goes on digesting on its own. It does not ask your advice, nor does it need any medical education, nor does it need any advice. It has simply an intrinsic wisdom of its own.

But it is just your house—you are not it. This house is going to become, one day, old. One day its walls will start dropping away, its doors falling. One day there will not be even a trace of the house—all will be gone. But what happened to the man who used to live in the house?

You have to understand that principle. You can call it awareness, enlightenment, consciousness, buddhahood—it doesn't matter what name you give to it. But it is the absolute responsibility of every human being not to waste time in mundane affairs. First things first! And the first thing is to be and to know what this being is. Don't go on running after butterflies. Don't go on looking at the horizon which only appears to be but is not.

I am reminded... Twenty-three centuries ago, Alexander the Great came to India. His teacher was a great philosopher, the father of logic, Aristotle. And when he was coming towards India, Aristotle asked him, "Can you bring something for me as a gift?"

Alexander said, "Anything—just say it."

Aristotle said, "It is not so easy, but I will wait. Please bring me a sannyasin when you come back, a man who has realized himself. Because we don't know what this means...what it means to be a

buddha. Get hold of a buddha and bring him with you."

Alexander was not aware of what he was promising. He said, "Don't be worried. If Alexander wants to move the Himalayas, they will have to move. And you are asking only about a human being. Just wait—within a few months I will be back."

And there was so much to do that he remembered only at the last moment that he had forgotten to catch hold of a buddha, of one who knows the innermost reality. He inquired on the borders of India as he was returning. People laughed at the very idea. They said, "In the first place, it is very difficult to recognize that somebody is a buddha. In the second place, if by chance you are open enough to receive the radiance of a buddha, you will fall down at his feet. You will forget all about taking him with you. We hope that you don't find a buddha —just go back home."

Alexander could not understand.... What kind of human being is a buddha, that he cannot be taken away by force? Finally, he said: "Send messengers all over the place, find out if there is somebody who proclaims that he has arrived home."

And people came, and they said, "Yes, one naked sannyasin standing by the side of the river says, 'Where else can I be?—I am here. And who else I can be?—I am the buddha.'"

Alexander went himself to meet the man. The dialogue was tremendously beautiful, but very shocking to Alexander the Great. He had never come across such a man because before he said a single word—he was holding a naked sword in his hand—the old man, naked, poor, said, "Put your sword back into its sheath, it will not be needed here. A man of intelligence carrying a sword? I will hit you! Just put the sword back into its sheath."

Alexander for the first time found somebody who could order him, and he had to follow. In spite of himself he had to follow. And he said, "I have come with a prayer: Just come with me, to my land. My teacher wants to see a buddha. In the West we don't know anything about what this inner self means."

The old man laughed. He said, "This is hilarious. If your teacher does not know, he is not even a teacher. And if he wants to see a buddha, he will have to come to a buddha; a buddha cannot be

carried to him. Just tell your teacher, 'If you are thirsty, come to the well; the well is not going to come to you.'"

"And as for you, Alexander," the old man said, "learn at least to be human. You introduced yourself as Alexander the Great. This is the ego that is preventing you from knowing your buddha. You are carrying it within yourself, but this 'greatness', this desire to conquer the world... What will you do with conquering the world? Soon death will take everything away. You will die naked, you will be buried in the earth. Nobody will bother not to tread over you, and you will not be even able to object, 'Keep away. I am Alexander the Great.' Please drop this idea of greatness. And also remember that the word 'Alexander' is not your name."

Alexander said, "My God! It is my name—how can I convince you?"

He said, "There is no question of convincing me. Nobody comes into the world with a name. All kinds of names are given—labels stuck, glued—and you become the label. You forget completely that you had come without any name, without any fame. And you will die in the same way.

"Tell your teacher to come here to face the lion. If he has the capacity to move inwards, only then can he know what it means to be a buddha; what it means to be enlightened. By somebody else becoming enlightened you cannot understand it—it is just like when somebody else drinks water it cannot quench your thirst."

Alexander touched the feet of the old man and said, "I am sorry to disturb you. Perhaps we don't understand each other's language at all."

And it is even today true: the Western mind and the Western educated mind—it may have been born in the East—has forgotten the language which Dōgen is going to use. You have to be very conscious, very alert, that you don't misunderstand. A different world, a different climate which used to be here, which had made this world a beautiful searching and seeking pilgrimage.... Now it is only a marketplace for purchasing arms, and fighting and killing and wars. Who bothers about meditation? It seems to be a very faraway echo. It does not seem to be related with us in any way. But unless

you are open to this faraway echo, you will not understand what Dōgen is saying.

Dōgen says:

When we look around our boat on the mountainless ocean, we see nothing but the circular shape of the ocean. But this large ocean is not circular or square; its other shapes and movements are innumerable. To fish it is like a palace. To celestial beings it is like a necklace. Only as far as the eye can reach, does it temporarily appear circular.

Its circularness is only an appearance. Although when you see it, it is there, you know that it is not a reality. If you go towards it you will never reach it; it will go on receding...it is the horizon. But it has a certain reality of its own, although it is not the ultimate reality. Our body is our circumference, our horizon. It appears, it lives, it breathes, yet it is not our very self.

This is also the case with all things. All things worldly and unworldly have various aspects, but we can see and realize them only through practical understanding.

For a blind man there is no light.

It happened... A very learned scholar was blind, in the times of Gautam Buddha. And he was so articulate in argumentation that the whole village was tortured by him, because everybody tried, "You are blind, that's why light is not within your reach."

But he said, "Then make it available through other sources. I can hear—beat it like a drum." You cannot beat light like a drum.

And the blind man said, "I can touch, at least let me touch light. My hand is open—where is your light? I can smell..," But all these senses are not capable of sensing the reality of light.

The whole village was tortured: "What to do with this man? He is so argumentative...we all know what light is, but he denies it. And he has valid reasons—we cannot offer any proof."

They heard that Gautam Buddha was coming to their village. They thought, "This is a good opportunity to take this blind man to Gautam Buddha. If Gautam Buddha cannot convince him then perhaps it is not possible. And either way it will be very crucial; we

can see how far Gautam Buddha can argue with this man."

But they were wrong. Gautam Buddha did not argue with the man. He simply said, "Don't harass him, it is ugly of you to tell him there is light. If you were compassionate enough you should have tried to find some physician to cure his eyes. Light is not an argument; you need eyes to see it and then there is no question of any doubt."

Gautam Buddha had his own personal physician. He told his physician, "You remain in this village until this man's eyes are cured. I will be moving with my caravan."

After six months the physician and the blind man came, but he was no more blind. He came dancing! He fell to the feet of Gautam Buddha and he said, "I am so grateful to you that you were not philosophical with me, that you did not humiliate me. That rather than making a great argumentation, you simply made a simple point: that it is not a question of light, it is a question of eyes."

The same is true about the inner self—it is not a question of your intelligence, not a question of your rationality, not a question of your logic, of your scientific knowledge, of your scriptures. It is a question of direct penetration with closed eyes into your own being, hidden behind your bones. Once that is known, a tremendous relaxation follows. Life for the first time becomes a dance. Even death is no more a disturbance.

However far fish sail in the water, there is no end to the water.
However far birds fly in the sky, there is no end to the sky. But neither of them has ever left the water or the sky.
It is an ancient story…about a very curious young fish inquiring, "I have heard so much about the ocean but I don't see where it is."

An old fish said to the young philosopher, "Don't be an idiot—we are in the ocean, and we *are* the ocean. We come out of it and we disappear into it. We are nothing but waves in the ocean."

The same is true about the birds. Do you think they can find the sky? Although they are flying all the day—faraway places—they cannot find the sky. Because they are born out of the sky and one day they will disappear into the sky.

These are symbolic statements. They are in fact saying that you are part of the universe. You arise like a wave in the universe and you disappear one day back into the universe. This universe is not something objective, it is something subjective. It is something that is connected with your innermost core. If you have found yourself you have found the whole ocean, the whole sky, with all its stars, with all its flowers, with all its birds. To find oneself is to find everything. And to miss oneself...you may have palaces and empires and great riches—all is futile.

When their need is great, there is great activity; when their need is small, there is little activity

The fish and the birds are spontaneous beings. Except man, in this whole universe nobody has gone insane. You go on working even though there is no need to work—keep busy, without any business, otherwise somebody will point out to you, "What are you doing?" And you don't have the courage to say, "I am just being."

People will laugh and they will suggest, "Do something, just being will not help. Get a job! Earn money." But a fish will not work more than is absolutely needed.

Henry Ford, before his death, was asked, "You have long before passed the line, broken all records of richness. Now there is no competitor against you. Why do you go on working continuously?"

And you will be surprised to know that he used to come to his office at seven o'clock every morning. The peons used to come at ten o'clock, the clerks at eleven, the manager at twelve. The manager would be gone by four, the clerks would be gone by five, the peons would be gone by six, but Henry Ford was still working. And he was the richest man of his times.

The questioner was right to ask him, "Why do you go on and on and on? It is unnecessary activity. You have earned so much, you could do anything you wanted."

And his answer is that of a wise man; unenlightened, but certainly life had made him wise. He said, "It just became a habit. I could not stop myself becoming more and more rich. I knew it was not needed any more, but it is very difficult to drop an old habit, a whole-life-long habit."

THE MOUNTAINLESS OCEAN

Except man...no trees have any habits, nor birds, nor fish. The whole nature is spontaneous. It simply functions when it is needed, it stops functioning and remains simply silent when it is not needed. In fact, according to me this is sanity: to do only that much as is needed. Even to go a single inch further and you have moved beyond sanity, you have become insane. And there is no end to insanity.

When their need is great, there is great activity. This can be understood from many aspects. Except man, no animal is interested in sex all the year round. There is a season, a mating season; once that season is gone...for the remainder of the year nobody bothers about sex. You will not find sex maniacs amongst birds, nor will you find celibates. You will not find, even in their mating season, that they are greatly happy.

I have been watching birds, animals, and I am amazed that their sexual activity seems to be a thing forced on them. They don't look happy. Just look at a dog making love. He is doing it under some compulsion, some biological compulsion, otherwise he is not interested. And once the season is gone there is no interest at all. That's why marriage has not appeared in the animal world. What will you do with a marriage? Once the mating season ends—good-bye to each other!

But with man it is a habit. He has turned even a biological necessity into a habit. You will be surprised to know that, according to psychologists and their surveys, every man is thinking about women at least once every four minutes, and every woman is thinking of men at least once every seven minutes. This disparity is the cause of tremendous misery.

That's why every night, when the husband comes home...the wife was perfectly okay, and suddenly she starts having a British face, she is suffering from a headache. Brilliant husbands bring super-strong Greek aspirins home with them. But there are very rarely brilliant husbands, because if you are brilliant you will never be a husband. That kind of thing is for the retarded, the brilliant remain absolutely free.

If you watch humanity, you will not believe that it is not a mad-

house. Somebody is smoking a cigarette...even though on the packet it is written it is dangerous to your life.

And just the other day, my ear was having a little ache. Anando was there. I asked her, "Can you bring a cotton-tip?"

She said, "No."

Now even on cotton-tips the same statement has been written, "It is dangerous to your health. Don't use them."

And Anando said to me, "Poor Hasya was saying that this was her only enjoyment, now even that is gone." Sitting silently and enjoying... It was not any harm to anybody.

There are people who are chewing gum. One cannot think of a more idiotic thing. Chewing gum? Gum is made for chewing?

People are doing all kinds of things that, if they watch and note them down, they will find.... "My God, these things I am doing, and people still think me sane." But everybody is keeping a mask and trying to hide every insanity behind it. You will see soon, when we meditate...because in meditation you have to put your mask away and let all the insanity of centuries come out. Don't hold it back, because it is a tremendous cleansing. And once you are a clean, clear consciousness your realization of buddhahood is not far away—perhaps just one step more.

Dōgen goes on:

Thus they never fail to express their full ability in each thing, and exert their free activity in each place.
But as soon as a bird leaves the sky, it dies. This is also the case when a fish leaves the water.

What about man? He has left his ocean long before. His oceanic relationship with existence is completely broken, there is no bridge left. And this is what is making him do all kinds of stupid things. In three thousand years, five thousand wars. One cannot believe that we are here just to kill each other. Isn't there anything more important than nuclear weapons?

Seventy percent of the whole humanity's income goes into war efforts. Even the poor countries, where they cannot afford food twice a day for their people, where they are living under the poverty line,

THE MOUNTAINLESS OCEAN

still they are wasting seventy percent of their income in creating bombs, in purchasing weapons. Do you think anything can be more insane than war?

A country like Germany, one of the most cultured, fell into the hands of a madman, Adolf Hitler. Nobody thinks about why it happened. Even a man like Martin Heidegger, perhaps the greatest philosopher in Germany, was a follower of Adolf Hitler. And Adolf Hitler was absolutely insane. He needed to be hospitalized.

But there must be something in every man to which he appealed. The whole Germany—with all its intelligence—became a victim. And you can see the stupidity. He said, "It is because of the Jews that Germany is not rising as a world power, otherwise it is our birthright to rule over the world. It is because of the Jews."

I have heard a small anecdote. The head rabbi of Berlin, on a morning walk, came across Adolf Hitler. It was a strange meeting, accidental; both had gone for a morning walk. Adolf Hitler recognized the head rabbi and he said, "Do you agree with me or not? What do you think is the cause that the German Nordic Aryans are not ruling all over the world?"

The rabbi said, "It is the bicycles. Destroy all bicycles and you will rule all over the world."

Adolf Hitler said, "Are you sane?"

He said, "As sane as you are. You have killed six million Jews on a pretext, without any reason."

Why did people become convinced that he was right about such a stupid thing, that the Jews were preventing Germany from becoming a great power? The Jews contributed wealth, intelligence, everything to Germany. You will be surprised to know that forty percent of Nobel Prizes go to the Jews.

But why did all the remaining Germans become convinced? It was out of jealousy. The Jews were rich, the Jews were intelligent, the Jews were always on top in everything.

It is very dangerous to be successful in an insane world because everybody wants to kill you—on any grounds; right or wrong, it does not matter. The whole of Germany became convinced, not because there was any argument or reason in Adolf Hitler's statements; but

53

because every German was jealous of the Jewish intelligence, their success, their wealth, their lifestyle. Because of this jealousy, Adolf Hitler managed for even the most intelligent Germans to act like animals.

Adolf Hitler alone killed thirty million people. And now the weapons Adolf Hitler used are just toys for children. Within these last forty years war technology has grown so much…and it is still in the hands of people like Ronald Reagan. It is in the hands of all kinds of politicians, and politicians are people who are psychologically sick. Just the very desire for power is sickness.

A healthy man wants to love—not to possess, not to dominate. A healthy man rejoices in life—does not go begging for votes. It is the people who are suffering from deep inferiority who want to have some power, to prove to themselves and to others that they are superior. The really superior person does not care a thing about power. He knows his superiority, he lives his superiority. In his songs, in his dances, in his poetry, in his paintings, in his music he lives his superiority. Only the inferior ones are left for politics.

What Dōgen is saying is, "Don't leave your sky, don't leave your water, don't leave your nature. Don't leave the existential. Because once you leave it you are just corpses moving around."

In the human world there are practice and enlightenment, or long life and short life. This is also the real state of things.

Don't be worried that you are not enlightened.

Dōgen is a very unique genius. He is saying, "You may be aware of your buddhahood or not aware of your buddhahood—don't be worried. When the right time and the right season come you will blossom into a buddha." Just wait…wait intelligently, wait without desire; enjoy waiting, make waiting itself a blissful silence, and whatever is your birthright is bound to flower. Nobody can prevent a bird from flying, nobody can prevent a cuckoo from singing, nobody can prevent a rose from blossoming. Who is preventing you from becoming buddhas? Except you, nobody is responsible for it.

Nevertheless, if a bird or fish tries to go through the sky or the water after knowing it completely, it will find no way to go along or no place to attain.

THE MOUNTAINLESS OCEAN

If you go into your inner world and into your inner sky you will not find any way or any end. You will find an eternal eternity, a pilgrimage without any beginning and without any end...an immortality, a deathlessness which suddenly transforms you totally without any effort, without any austerity, without torturing yourself. You are already what you want to be, just a small thing is missing—very small. Wake up! In your waking you are a buddha. In your sleep you remain a buddha, but you are not aware of it.

When one person becomes a buddha he knows that everybody else is a buddha. Somebody is sleeping, somebody is snoring, somebody is running after a woman, somebody is doing some other kind of stupidity—but buddhas are buddhas. Even if you are smoking a cigarette, it does not mean that you have lost your essentiality; it only shows your sleep and nothing else.

A poet has written:

> *Taking hold, one is astray in*
> *nothingness;*
> *Letting go, the Origin is regained.*

Letting go, relaxing, settling into yourself, the origin is regained.

> *Since the music stopped, no*
> *shadow's touched*
> *My door: again the village moon*
> *is above the river.*

Even if you become enlightened, only your vision changes, otherwise everything remains the same. Of course, the rose is more beautiful than it used to be. Just because all the dust from your mirror is missing, the world becomes a paradise.

...*My door: again the village moon*
is above the river...reflecting in the river.

The more you become clean of your thoughts which are just dust, the more you become reflective. And the day you can reflect the whole existence in its purity you have arrived home.

Another poem:

> Scoop up the water, and the
> moon is in your hands;
> Hold the flowers, and your
> clothes are scented with them.

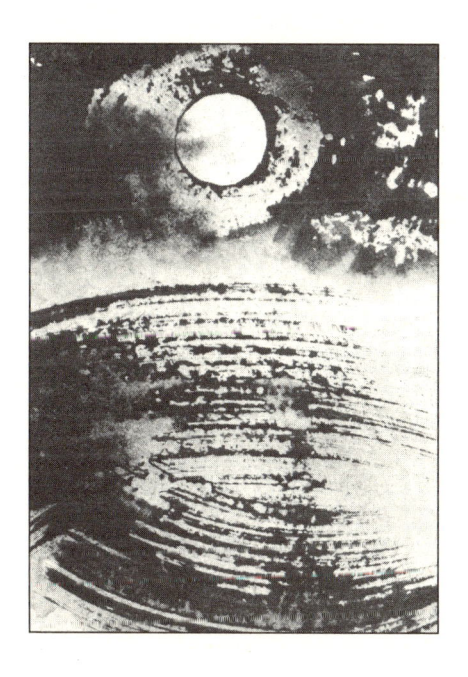

This is something tremendously beautiful. Zen speaks the language of poetry. What the poet is trying to say is that if you come across a buddha—you may know it or not—some fragrance of the buddha and his presence will be caught by your being.

It was a usual practice in Zen that seekers continued moving from one master to another master until the moment they found a man whose very presence fulfilled them; in whose presence all their masks and defenses fell down, in whose presence they became suddenly naked, just-born, innocent. Then this was the sign that you had found your master.

Bashō wrote:

> *Skylark*
> *sing all day,*
> *and day not long enough.*

He is saying that you work the whole day, your whole life, never knowing the splendor of your being because your work—your so-called mundane activities—takes all your time. Life is so short, seventy years pass so quickly... You don't know even when your childhood becomes your youth, you don't know when your youth disappears and you become old, you don't know that you are moving continuously towards the grave. Whatever you do, the grave is coming closer.

Remember, life is short, but it has become too short because of your unnecessary activity. I am surprised at people who are playing cards or chess, or going to the movie. And if you ask them, "What are you doing?" they say they are killing time. As if too much time, superfluous, has been given to them and they are killing it by playing cards. Just look at people leaning on the chess board as if it is their life, standing in a line before a movie house...

I used to know a man...he was the father of one of my friends. In my village there was only one movie hall. I saw that old man going every day, at exactly the same time, to the movie hall. And a film was shown at least for five or seven days, or more than that. It was not a big place. But he would see it every day for seven days.

Finally, I had to interrupt him. I said, "This is too much. Are you mad? You go on seeing the same film every day."

He said, "How to kill time? I am retired, just waiting for death. I think it does not matter, one day more...just go to see the movie. What else is one supposed to do when one is retired?"

"And anyway," he said, "everybody is doing the same thing again and again and again, so don't think that I am crazy."

I said, "No, you are not crazy, you are just a specimen of this whole humanity."

I have heard about one man in California—Avirbhava, take

DŌGEN

note—who married ten times. Because in California human craziness has come to its peak. All the surveys show that everything in California lasts, at the most, three years. Everything is fashion: marriage, job, city, house, car—everything. Within three years one is bored, wants to change to something else.

And this man married ten times. The tenth time, after two days, he realized, "This woman seems to be one that I have married before."

In fact all women are just different brands of cars—just the bonnet differs. Somebody has a longer nose, somebody has a shorter nose... But the strange thing is, people go on exploring the same territory again and again and again. And still people think they are sane.

Another Zen poem:

> *Wind subsiding,*
> *the flowers still fall;*
> *Birds crying, the mountain*
> *silence*
> *deepens.*

These are actual experiences of meditations, which have become condensed in haikus.

Wind subsiding,
the flowers still fall;
Birds crying, the mountain
silence
deepens.

This must be a man of meditation...sitting silently by the side of the mountain, watching whatever is happening. Meditation is, in essence, becoming a watcher on the hills.

Maneesha has asked:

> Our Beloved Master,
> *It's easy enough to feel totally content in Your presence and enjoy Your enlightenment; it's also easy enough to work oneself up into a state of*

panic about what we must do to realize our own enlightenment. Isn't the art of being with a master having the contentment and thirst running like an undercurrent throughout one simultaneously?

Maneesha, a single experience is enough, it lasts for eternity. I am not referring to intellectual experiences. You can intellectually feel that you have relaxed. When I take you inwards, certainly you close your eyes. But when I say to you, "Be silent," your mind still goes on and on, weaving a thousand and one things. You feel a certain silence...but it will be lost. And when I say to you, "Let go," you try, but you try very carefully. You look on both sides, on whom you are falling, whether it is worth falling. You take every care that no fracture happens. But in this very care you miss the point of let-go.

Enlightenment is worth multiple fractures. When you let go, let go. When you laugh, then become laughter. When you are silent, be silent. When I say, "Go in"—search inwards. Forget the body and forget the world.

I even tell you to die. You make every effort, but for dying no effort is needed. You just lie down there waiting for Nivedano's beat so that you can wake up again. Not a single one remains dead just a little while more, everybody immediately...it is all intellectual. If it was not intellectual, every day we would have to call an ambulance because this place would become a graveyard. But nobody dies. In the whole world people are dying, except in this Buddha Hall where we are trying to die every day. On the contrary, you come back healthier, more robust.

Maneesha, what you feel is still intellectual. You are intelligent enough to feel it, but intellect is not going to give you the right experience; it blocks. You need not try to use the mind, in any way. Let it happen spontaneously. You simply risk yourself totally. Then even if you die, what does it matter? One day you are going to die, and this day is perfectly good. There are only seven days. You will have to die on Monday, on Tuesday, on Saturday, on Sunday... What does it matter?

But if you die really, leaving the mind and body aside, you will come to know your immortality; you will see the fiction of death.

DŌGEN

Death has never happened, you have only changed your form. And those few who have realized it have not even moved into another form, they have moved into the eternal ocean, into the very existence itself, losing themselves completely. That is the ultimate ecstasy.

Before somebody dies...particularly Sardar Gurudayal Singh is getting ready. He has been missing every day, perhaps today he is going to die. We promise him we will celebrate...don't be worried.

Gorgeous Gloria is very excited as she plans her coming wedding, with her friend, Sherry Cherry.

"Have you heard about the secret aphrodisiac from India?" asks Sherry.

"Why, no," says Gloria. "What is it?"

"It is called 'Burnt *bindhi*,'" says Sherry. "And if you want an unforgettable wedding night, get him to eat a dozen burnt *bindhis* after the ceremony."

A week later, Gloria meets Sherry in the supermarket.

"How did the wedding night go?" asks Sherry.

"Oh, okay I guess," says Gloria. "But only eight of the *bindhis* worked!"

In a little town in the Wild West of America, Polly Peckin, the pretty young tourist, is intrigued by a big macho-looking Indian. She is watching him and has noticed that he says, "Chance!" to every passing female.

Finally, Polly's curiosity gets the better of her and she walks up to him and says, "Hello."

To which he answers, "Chance!"

"That's interesting," says Polly. "I thought all Indians said, 'How!'"

"I know *how*," he replies. "Just want chance!"

Swami Deva Coconut arrives in Bombay airport with his pet parrot on his shoulder. He is intercepted by an Indian customs official who says, "Hey, stop! You have got to pay import duty on that parrot!"

"How much?" asks Coconut.

"Let me see," says the official, paging through his imports book.

"Here we are," he continues. "Five hundred rupees for an alive parrot, one hundred rupees for a stuffed one."

"Hey, Coconut," screams the parrot. "Don't get any crazy ideas!"

Swami Bharti Barfi, one of Shree Rajneesh's Indian disciples, is sitting on an Air India plane with the Shankaracharya of Puri and some of his aides. They are cruising at thirty-five thousand feet over the Indian sub-continent, when the shankaracharya suddenly feels very generous.

"If I throw this hundred-rupee note out the window," he says, "I will make one harijan very happy."

One of his aides adds, "But if you throw out two fifty-rupee notes, you will make two people happy."

And the other aide says, "Well, why not throw out one hundred one-rupee notes, and make one hundred people happy?"

At this point Swami Bharti Barfi stands up and says, "Why don't you make nine hundred million people happy and throw *yourself* out the window?"

Okay Nivedano...give the first beat, and everybody goes crazy.

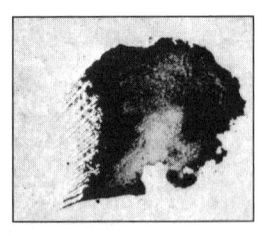

Nivedano...

Be silent...
close your eyes...
no movement of the body—feel frozen.
Go inwards, deeper...and deeper,
just like an arrow.
Penetrate all the layers
and hit the center of your existence.
This silence...
this peace...
Start discovering the buddha within you.
You are just a rock...
non-essential parts have to be taken away,
and the buddha statue will reveal itself.

Nivedano...

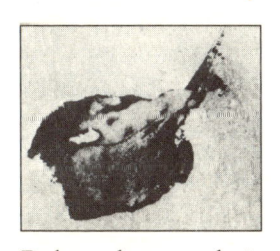

Relax...let go...die!
In this moment,
at the very center of your being,
you are the immortal buddha.
You don't have to pray.
You don't have to worship.

You don't have to go to any temple.
Because you are the temple of the buddha.
Realize it
and express it in every action—
the grace of it, the beauty of it,
the blissfulness of it,
the ecstasy of it.
And your whole life becomes a dancing flame
of immortal joy.
This is the dimension
the whole East has devoted itself to
for millions of years:
to discover the point which is unmovable,
which is the very center of the cyclone.
Rejoice in it,
and remember the path,
how you have reached to it,
so that whenever you want,
you close your eyes
and immediately the buddha is there.

Nivedano...

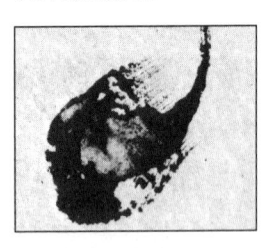

Come back from your death…
to life eternal.
Sit down for a few moments
just like a buddha,
in all his glory and splendor.
These few moments make this place the most
precious in the whole world.

Ten thousand buddhas
melting and merging into each other,
just like waves of the ocean.
The world has forgotten this language...
it has to be reminded.
Everyone has to become a message,
not a missionary.
Revealing your own buddhahood
is enough to wake up people around you.
Your joy,
your blissfulness,
your benediction has to be shared.
The more you share it,
the more you have it.

Okay, Maneesha?
Yes, Beloved Master.

Can we celebrate the gathering
of ten thousand buddhas?
Yes, Beloved Master.

DIVE A LITTLE DEEP

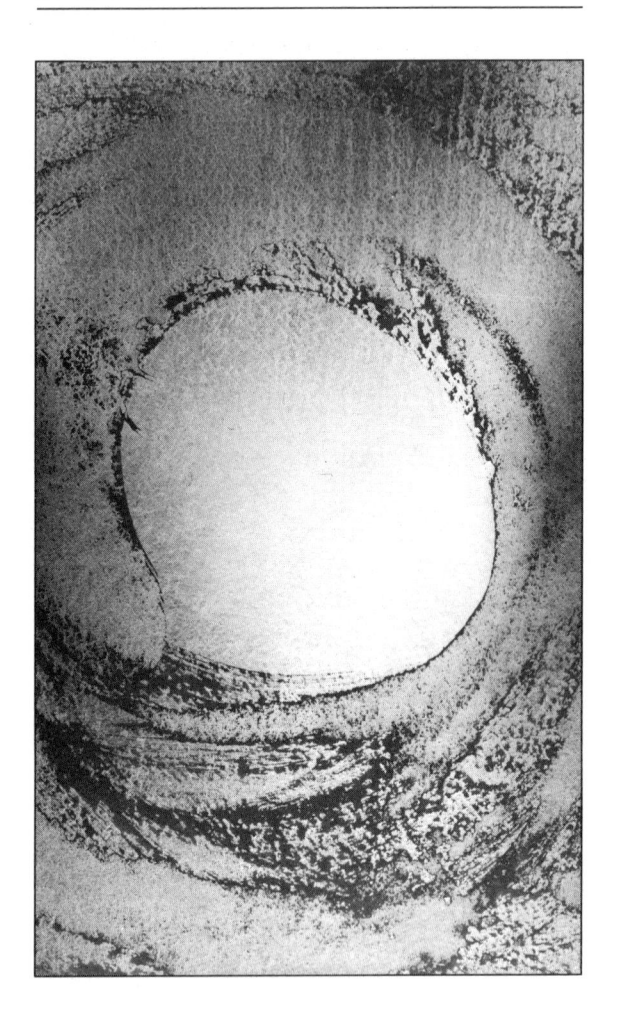

The thief
left it behind—
the moon at the window.

*Our Beloved Master,
Dōgen said:*
In the practice of the highest supreme wisdom, it is most difficult to meet prominent masters. Whether men or women, they must be those who have realized something indescribable ... This is the realization of the essence of the Way. Therefore, they lead and benefit others, setting aside no causality or making no difference between the self and others.

Once we have met a master, we must practice the Way, aloof from worldly relations and grudging a spare time, even in thinking, non-thinking and neutral thinking. Therefore, we should train ourselves as single-heartedly as if we were saving our head from a burning fire. A Zen master who has dropped away his body and mind is none other than ourselves.

It is inevitably by sincerity and piety that we realize and receive the essence of our master's Law. These qualities neither come from outside nor rise from inside, but from attaching more importance to the Law than to our body, or from renouncing the world and entering the Way. If we attach a little more importance to our body than to the Law,

we shall be unable to realize and receive the Way.

....When someone has realized the great Law and the essence of the Buddhas and patriarchs, we serve him, reverently prostrating ourselves....

Sakyamuni-buddha said: "When you meet a master who expounds the supreme wisdom, do not consider his birth, look at his appearance, nor dislike his faults or worry about his behavior. Rather, out of respect for his great Wisdom, treat him with a large sum of money or celestial meals and flowers, or reverently prostrate yourself before him three times a day, giving him no cause for worry; and you will surely find the supreme bodhi-wisdom."

Dōgen continued, ...Both men and women can realize the Way. In any case, the realization of the Way should be respected, regardless of sex. This is an extremely excellent rule in the Way.... Even a little girl of seven can become the teacher of the four classes of Buddhists...if she practices and realizes the Law... We should make a venerative offering to her as if to the Buddhas.

This is a traditional manner in Buddhism. I feel sorry for those who have never known or received it personally.

Maneesha, it is one of the most ancient problems—how to recognize the master? Because without the master there is almost no way. I say almost, because perhaps one person in a million may reach to the truth without the master. But it is just accidental, it cannot be made a rule, it is just an exception that simply proves the rule.

And the great concern of masters has been to explain to people the ways of recognizing the master, because the master is the Way. Unless you have seen someone self-realized, you will not trust yourself that you can be realized. Once you have seen a buddha, an enlightened one, a tremendous flame suddenly starts blossoming in you, "If this beauty, this grace, this wisdom, this blissfulness can happen to any man, then why can it not happen to me?"

As far as human beings are concerned, we have the same seeds and the same potentiality. But a seed can remain a seed and may never become a flower, although there was every possibility available. But rather than disappearing in the soil, the seed can remain

safe, hiding in a stone cave, thinking that it is too rainy outside, worrying that it is too sunny outside, fearing the unknown. It feels cozy in the closed silence of the cave, but there it cannot grow, there it will simply get rotten. There it will simply remain something...it could have been a beautiful manifestation, it simply remains unmanifested, a song unsung, a poetry unwritten, a life unlived.

It is very essential to find a man who can provoke in you the challenge to attain to your heights. The master is nothing but a challenge—if it has happened to me, it can happen to you. And the authentic master—there are so many teachers propounding doctrines, beliefs, philosophies—the authentic master is not concerned with words; is not concerned with beliefs, atheism or theism; is not concerned even with God, or heaven and hell. The authentic master is concerned only with one single thing—to provoke you to see your potentiality, to see inwards. His presence makes you silent, his words deepen your silence, his very being slowly starts melting your falseness, your mask, your personality.

What is the problem of the seed? It is the problem of you, too. The problem of the seed is that the cover is protective. In losing the cover it becomes vulnerable. The seed is perfectly happy covered, but it does not know that there are more skies beyond skies to be discovered, that unless it goes to the beyond it has not lived; because it has not known the world of stars, and it has not lived as a flower dancing in the rain and in the sun and in the wind, it has not heard the music of existence. It remained closed in its safety and security.

And exactly the same is the problem with man. Every man is a bodhisattva. The word 'bodhisattva' means, in essence a buddha. The distance between a bodhisattva and a buddha is the distance between the seed and the flower. It is not much, it just takes a little courage to bridge the distance.

But hidden in the darkness of a cave, who is going to give you the encouragement? Who is going to pull you out from your security? The master's function is to give you a taste of insecurity, to give you a taste of openness. And once you know that openness, insecurity.... They are basic ingredients of freedom, without them you cannot open your wings and fly in the sky of infinity.

DIVE A LITTLE DEEP

It is absolutely essential to avoid the teachers, they are fake masters. It is very difficult, because they speak the same language. So you have not to listen to the words, you have to listen to the heart; you have not to listen to their doctrines, their logic and arguments, you have to listen to their grace, their beauty, their eyes; you have to listen to and feel the aura that surrounds a master. Just like a cool breeze it touches you. Once you have found your master, you have found the key to open the treasure of your potentialities.

Dōgen is talking about this ancient and eternal problem. Dōgen says:

In the practice of the highest supreme wisdom, it is most difficult to meet prominent masters.

It is difficult, and if it was difficult in Dōgen's time it has become more difficult nowadays. The world has become more worldly, education has become irreligious, science predominates—and science does not believe in the insight of your being. Our whole culture for the first time in history is absolutely materialistic. It does not matter whether you are in the East or in the West, the same educational pattern has spread all over the globe.

Although you may go traditionally, formally—just as a social conformity—to the temple, to the mosque, deep down you don't have any trust, deep down there is only doubt. Deep down you are going into the temple not because of any realization, not because you have to show your gratitude to God. You are going there out of fear of the society in which you live—you don't want to be an outcast. It is simply a social conformity.

It became very clear when in 1917 the Soviet Union went through a revolution. Before the revolution Russia was one of the most orthodox countries in the world. All kinds of superstitions were believed, there were many saints, a great hierarchy in the church. It was absolutely independent from the Vatican, it had its own church. But after the revolution, just within five years, all those beliefs, cultivated for centuries, disappeared. Nobody bothered any more about God.

That does not mean that everybody had understood that there is no God. That simply means the society had changed and you have to

change with society—another social conformity. I don't belive in Russian atheists, just as I don't believe in any theists, Hindu, Christian or Mohammedan; for the simple reason that their religion is not their own experience, is not their own love affair, it is just a conformity to remain respectable in the crowd.

What is your religion except conformity?

By conformity nobody has found religion. Today it has become almost a universal conformity, because science overrules the mind, logic prevails on our thinking, logic denies anything irrational, science denies anything eternal. Obviously it has become more and more difficult to find an authentic master. Even to find a teacher is difficult because that too has become out of date. A teacher will be talking about the *Upanishads*, will be talking about the *Bible*, will be talking about the *Torah*, will be talking about the *Koran*—all are out of date.

Do you think a newspaper twenty centuries afterwards will have any significance? Just within one day its significance is finished. In the morning you were waiting so curiously for the newspaper, by the evening it is thrown out. It has served its purpose: a curiosity to know what is happening around, just a new and more technical way of gossiping.

Now it is no more possible to continue the old type of gossiping because people are living so far away from each other. Newspapers, radio and television are the new forms of gossiping. They spread all kind of nonsense and stupidity to people. This used to be the work of the priest, of the teacher.

Even in the past, as Dōgen says, it was very difficult to meet prominent masters. But they have never ceased to be. Even today it is possible, although it has become more difficult to find a master. Because the whole world and its climate, its mind, has turned away from the inner search. One who goes into the inner search today goes alone, without any support from the society. In fact the society creates all kinds of problems for the man who is going in search of himself.

People simply laugh, "Don't be foolish, go in search of money, go in search of a beautiful woman, go in search of becoming the richest man in the world, go in search of being the prime minister of a country.

DIVE A LITTLE DEEP

Where are you going and what will you do even if you find yourself? You will be simply stuck. Once you have found yourself then what are you going to do? You cannot eat it. It is just useless." The whole endeavor of the centuries has suddenly become completely useless, because so very few people have dared to cross the line, the boundary that the society creates around you.

These few people have found the very source of life, they have found that we are not born with our birth, and we are not going to die with our death. Neither birth nor death...our essence is eternal, beginningless, endless. Births and deaths have happened a thousand-and-one times, they are just episodes, very small things compared to our eternity.

Whenever anybody finds this eternity, it starts transforming him. He becomes a new man in the sense that his vision is clear. He does not belong to any crowd, he cannot be a Christian or a Hindu or a Mohammedan; because he knows in his innermost core that we are all part of one existence. All divisions are stupid. How can a man who has realized himself belong to a crowd, be a member of a crowd? He becomes a peak of consciousness, standing alone like the Everest. He is enough unto himself, and to find him is certainly difficult, but not impossible. You can make it impossible if you go on your search with certain prejudices, with certain criteria already decided by your mind.

For example, a Jaina, even if he comes across a buddha, will not be able to see him. His eyes are covered with his so-called Jainism. He can respect only a man like Mahavira, that is his criterion. And the trouble is, every realized soul is so unique you cannot make criteria. You will have to be more subtle, more intelligent. The Jaina cannot accept Buddha as self-realized because he still wears clothes. His idea of self-realization is that one renounces everything, even clothes; one stands naked.

But please remember, even an actor can stand naked, don't make it a criterion. Mahavira is unique—he loves to be naked, in the open air, under the sky and the stars. It is beautiful but it is not a criterion. Gautam Buddha eats once a day. Now that is not a criterion, that if somebody eats twice a day he cannot be understood as a buddha. But

even our so-called intelligent and our so-called religious people like Mahatma Gandhi make such stupid criteria.

According to him a man of realization cannot drink tea. All the Buddhist masters have been drinking tea, it has been their discovery. It was Bodhidharma who discovered tea. The name 'tea' comes from the mountain Tha in China, where Bodhidharma was meditating. And the name has remained the same in different languages...just slight changes. In Hindi it is *chai*, in Marathi it is *cha*, in Chinese it is *tha*, in English it has become tea. But a thousand masters have never denied tea as something unspiritual.

On the contrary, Zen has in its monasteries a special teahouse, and when they go for tea it is called a tea ceremony. They have transformed the simple act of drinking tea into a beautiful meditation. You have to leave your shoes outside as if you are entering into a temple. And there is a master who is going to lead the ceremony. Then everybody sits down in the silence of the monastery, the tea is prepared on the samovar and everybody listens to the music of the samovar boiling the tea. It becomes a meditation. Watchfulness is meditation, what you watch does not matter.

Then the master with great grace brings the tea to everybody; pours the tea with immense awareness, consciousness, carefulness, respectfulness, and everybody receives the tea as if something divine is being received. In that silence sipping the tea...and this very ordinary thing has become a spiritual experience. Nobody can speak in the teahouse, silence is the rule. When you put down your cups and saucers you also bow down with gratitude to existence. The tea was only a symbol.

But in Mahatma Gandhi's ashram you could not drink tea, you could not fall in love with a woman. Every day you had to eat with your meal neem leaves, which are the bitterest leaves in the world, just to destroy your taste; because scriptures say that tastelessness is a criterion of spirituality. It can be a criterion of stupidity, it cannot be a criterion of spirituality; otherwise all buffalos will be spiritual.

Have you watched buffalos? They always chew the same grass, showing in no way whether they are happy or unhappy, remaining so content and aloof. And the whole day it continues, chewing and

DIVE A LITTLE DEEP

chewing. It cannot be very delicious. You can try, once in a while it is good to try what other species around the world are doing. But I will not say that tastelessness has anything to do with religion. On the contrary, the more you become meditative, the more your taste becomes deeper. Every sense becomes more sensitive, you hear more, you see better, your touch starts becoming warmer.

Just touch a few people's hands and you will see the difference. Some people's hands are warm. The warm hands show that they are ready to give, to share; the warmth is their energy moving towards you, it is really a love symbol. But holding some people's hands will be just like holding a dead branch of a tree, nothing moves in their hands. But these people in the past have been called spiritual. The more dead you are the more spiritual. Don't eat for the taste's sake!

You cannot believe that Buddhist scriptures have thirty-three thousand rules for a person to be spiritual. At least I cannot become spiritual, just because I cannot count that many rules. I cannot remember that much—thirty-three thousand rules! Whenever I count, I count on my fingers and after the third finger I always get lost. But that does not mean that I cannot be spiritual, arithmetic has nothing to do with spirituality. And what are those rules?

One instance I will give to you. A young monk is going to spread Buddha's word to the masses. Before taking his leave he touches Buddha's feet and asks him if he has something to say to him, because he will not be able to see him again until the second monsoon comes.

Buddha said, "Yes, I have a few instructions for you. One thing is, never look more than four feet ahead of you."

The man said, "But why?"

Buddha said, "It is to avoid women. At the most you can see their feet. Then just move on, don't look at their face. Keep your eyes glued to the ground."

Now such a man cannot see the stars, such a man cannot see the sunset or the sunrise, such a man is utterly cut off from existence, his sensitivity has been killed. He has eyes but he is almost blind—eyes that can see only four feet ahead. His tremendous capacity for seeing is reduced to only four feet.

The young monk asked, "If once in a while I forget, or if there is

73

some special situation in which I have to see a woman, what should I do?"

Buddha said, "Close your eyes. I am especially concerned, because once you have seen a beautiful woman you can close your eyes but you cannot forget the face." In fact with closed eyes she becomes more beautiful.

If I were in the place of Gautam Buddha I would give everybody a magnifying glass! Carry it! Whenever you come across a beautiful woman, just look and then her eyes will look like monsters; her nose will become so big that no Jew could defeat it. But this is not spirituality, carrying a magnifying glass...

His restriction is nothing but repression, and a repressed person can never enter into his own being. Those repressed feelings and thoughts become a hard shell dividing him from himself, from his own origin. Only an unrepressed, thoughtless, silent being can break away the barrier and reach to his living source. And the moment you reach your living source...you don't have to do anything, it does miracles. It starts changing your attitudes, your approaches, it starts changing everything that you have known about yourself. It brings to you a new beinghood.

To find a master is easy if you are available not only to words, but to silences too; not only to words because the truth never comes through words, but between the words, between the lines, in the silent spaces. If you are searching for a master don't carry any criterion, any prejudice. Be absolutely available, so that when you come across a master you can feel his energy. He carries a whole world of energy around him. His own experience radiates all around him. If you are open and not afraid of experiencing a new thing, of tasting something original, it is not very difficult to find a master. What difficulty there is, is on your side.

But Dōgen's statement is right:

...it is most difficult to meet prominent masters. Whether men or women, they must be those who have realized something indescribable.

That's what makes them masters: if they know something which cannot be described, if they have some experience which cannot be explained. The master is a mystery. He knows it but he cannot say it. He

DIVE A LITTLE DEEP

can share it if you are ready. He can invite you into his own very being. If you are unafraid and fearless, courageous enough to explore the most unknown part of existence, you can become a guest in the master's home. But remember, the moment you enter into the master's home the master enters into you. Two consciousnesses cannot remain separate. Once two consciousnesses come close they become one.

And this is the only thing that has to be remembered: if with someone you feel a deep affinity, a deep synchronicity, as if one soul is in two bodies, then don't miss this man. He is going to lead you to the same incredible, indescribable, inexpressible experience.

This is the realization of the essence of the Way.
Finding the master is finding the Way.

Therefore, they lead and benefit others, setting aside no causality
or making no difference between the self and others.

A very famous Sufi mystic used to come to a place where I lived for twenty years, and his disciples always wanted me to meet their master. I said, "The only way is: next time your master can stay with me."

So the next time the Sufi master came he stayed with me, and I asked him first thing, "Are you still Mohammedan?"

He looked surprised and shocked. He said, "Of course."

I said, "Then you don't know the indescribable. These divisions between Mohammedans and Hindus and Jainas and Buddhists are divisions of the mediocre and retarded."

But he said, "I realized God. I see him."

I said, "It is all nonsense."

Anando has just brought to me... There is in America a new species of priests, television priests, that has never existed before. A very famous television priest has become more famous since he has declared that he sees God every night. God is nine hundred feet long! I told Anando, "Write a letter to him from me, 'Please tell me, do you carry a ladder and something to measure with? or is it just guess work?'" Nine hundred feet, exactly!

We think we live in the twentieth century. Even in America people are not living in the twentieth century, to say nothing of countries like India. Millions worship that man and nobody even bothers that this is so stupid.

Seeing this, another missionary started declaring that he also sees God and he has a long white beard. So I have sent him my picture, "You don't be deceived, it is me who visits you in your dreams! In the first place, if God is eternal he cannot have white hair. He will always be young. It is man who becomes old."

He has even published his picture, which is similar to mine, so I have told him, "Just look at my picture. Just not to be recognized by everybody else I'm wearing the glasses. But it's me you have been seeing in your dreams. Don't exploit people by saying that you are seeing God."

God is not an object. You cannot see God. God is your very consciousness. It is the seer, not the seen. It is *you*, not some object somewhere. It is your innermost center, which is the only eternal point, unchangeable, immortal, divine in its beautitude, in its blessings.

When you come close to a master just remember one thing: withdraw all defenses. Be as empty as possible, so that the master's energy can penetrate you, can penetrate your being, can touch your heart. And it is an immediate realization. Just as when you fall in love, you don't think about love, you don't consult librarians about love, you don't ask your elders how to fall in love. There is no school that teaches how to fall in love. But people fall in love, it suddenly happens.

Just as love suddenly happens on the lower level, on the physical and biological level...finding the master is a form of the highest love. The moment you come into the area of his influence—which is called the buddhafield, the field of the master—you suddenly start throbbing with a new energy, you suddenly feel a new freshness, a new breeze passing through you, a new song which makes no sound. All that is left for you is to relax in deep gratitude. Don't even utter the word 'thank you', because that is separating. This is not the time to utter a word...just a gesture of gratitude.

Once we have met a master, we must practice the Way. If the master himself is the Way, how do you practice? You simply watch how the master moves, what gestures he makes, how he responds to situations. Because he is every moment an absolute awareness. His every action is an indication of his innermost being. Watch him! Watch

him when he is sleeping, watch him when he is waking, watch him when he is talking, watch him when he is sitting silently, doing nothing.

Watching the master with deep gratitude and love, absorbing his energy silently.... It is almost like drinking water when you are thirsty, a deep feeling of contentment comes to you.

...aloof from worldly relations and grudging a spare time, even in thinking, non-thinking and neutral thinking. Therefore, we should train ourselves as singleheartedly as if we were saving our head from a burning fire. A Zen master who has dropped away his body and mind is none other than ourselves.

The buddha and you in your deepest consciousness are one. The *Upanishads* declare: *Aham brahmasmi*—I am God. It is not out of any egoistic attitude—those people who wrote the Upanishads have not even signed it. We don't know who wrote those Upanishads. Their statements are so clear—it is impossible to have an ego and make such clear-cut statements about the truth. And when they declared, "Aham brahmasmi," they were not declaring it for themselves only; they were declaring for everybody, "You are the God." Don't search for him anywhere else. You will not find him in any holy place. If you cannot find him within yourself, you cannot find him anywhere else. The moment you find him in you, he is everywhere. Then you will see him in the song of a cuckoo or the chirping of the birds or in a thunderbolt or in this silence. Then he is everywhere.

Once you know him within you, you know him all over. The whole existence becomes one continent. The ego makes you small islands. And remember, no man is an island, because even the small island deep down is joined with the continent. Just one has to go a little deep, dive a little deep.

It is inevitably by sincerity and piety that we realize and receive the essence of our master's Law.

This word 'Law' is a very difficult translation of the word *dhamma*. It gives a distorted view; the moment you hear the word 'law' you remember your courts and constitution, your legal authorities; you don't remember the word 'dhamma'.

Dhamma is a Pali translation of the Sanskrit *dharma*. And 'dharma'

means: fire is hot—hot is the dhamma of fire; ice is cold, it is the dhamma of ice. And you are a buddha, it is the dhamma of you. Better translated, law should not be used as a translation for dhamma, but rather 'nature'. It is your nature to be a buddha. It does not matter that sometimes you forget. You can remain in forgetfulness for your whole life or many lives. Still, as an undercurrent the same dhamma, the same buddha, the same consciousness continues.

Once it happened... George Bernard Shaw was traveling to some place from London. The ticket checker came and George Bernard Shaw looked into everything, searched his whole suitcase, perspiring. The ticket was not found, although he knew perfectly well that he had purchased a ticket. The ticket checker said, "Don't be worried. I know you, everybody knows you. You must have put it somewhere. Don't be worried. I will take care that nobody harasses you."

Bernard Shaw said, "That is not the problem, my boy. The ticket is not the problem. The problem is how to know where I am going. Do you think I am searching for the ticket for you?"

You can forget. Forgetfulness is part of our nature, just as remembrance is. Sometimes you all must have come to a point where you were trying to remember some old acquaintance's name. You say it is just on the tip of the tongue. What do you mean? If it is on the tip of the tongue, spit it out! You know perfectly well that you know, but it is not coming to expression. The harder you try the more difficult it will become, because the harder you try, the more narrow the passage becomes. Mind becomes tense and old memories cannot get through that tenseness. Finally you give up and just start smoking, and while smoking suddenly it comes. You cannot believe, you had been trying so hard, you knew it was just on the tip of the tongue, and still you could not express it. I say to you the buddha is just on the tip of your tongue. It is only a question of smoking a little. A little relaxation, that's what the smoking gives.

People smoke cigarettes and cigars not knowing that psychologically it is simply their mother's breast. That's why it gives them so much relaxation. From the nipple of the mother's breast lukewarm milk comes to the child; from the cigarette lukewarm smoke comes in—and you have forgotten everything, you have become again

DIVE A LITTLE DEEP

a child, innocent, relaxed. No government can stop people from smoking, because smoking is not really the question. It has a deep psychology behind it.

You can see the psychology without much erudition. Poets sing about the women's breast more than anything else. Painters paint the woman's breast more than anything else. There are a few painters who only paint women's breasts and nothing else. They go on improving...

Why this obsession? Why this fixation? The reality is that more and more mothers are not willing to breast feed the child, because to feed the child this way is to misshape the breast. The child goes on pulling, it makes the breast longer, and every woman wants the breast to be shapely, round, a full moon, and these young monsters won't allow it. They are interested in their work, because a round breast, a sculptor's idea of a woman's breast, will kill the child. If the breast is round the child cannot have his nourishment, his nose will be closed. Either he can breathe or he can drink; both together he cannot do. So all those Khajuraho paintings and statues, all those great painters, don't understand that the poor child's life is at stake!

Every woman becomes interested, and now it is even being discussed in parliaments around the world, "Should women be forced to feed the child, or should they be given the freedom to choose themselves?" No woman wants to distort her breasts. Unless they find some technological device...and it can be done. Just join the breast and the baby's mouth with a small pipe. And the child is almost on a cigar from the very beginning!

I always see simple solutions to very great problems! Just a small plastic pipe...the child will enjoy it and he can continue to enjoy it later on also because he is going to be in companionship with women.

Nobody can prevent by law something which has a psychological root. And nobody can prevent you from becoming a buddha, because it is your very nature. It is another matter that you get involved in the small things of the world—power, prestige, respectability—and you forget to give some time to yourself. Just a little time to yourself, forgetting the whole world...there is no need to renounce it. I am against renouncing anything.

All the religions of the world have been religions of renunciation.

They wanted people to meditate, to renounce the world, to go to the mountains, to the forests, to the deserts where nobody comes along. But that did not work, it does not work. Even if you go to the mountain a crowd will follow you there—in your mind, not outside. Outside you will not see anybody, but with your eyes closed you will think about so many things: your wife, your children, your old parents, your friends and all kinds of stupid things—Lions Club and Rotary Club. Things that you have never thought of before will start coming to your mind, because having nothing else to chew...even chewing gum is not available, you have to chew something. People start thinking of strange things.

But this is not realizing oneself. I am against renouncing the world, I want you to be in the world as totally as possible. So just once in a while be on a holiday. Just in the early morning for a few moments renounce everything, forget everything, and just be yourself. In the dark night when everybody is asleep sit on your bed and just be yourself.

This is far more successful. The old renunciation was almost violent. Nobody has pointed it out because nobody wants to be condemned, but I am so much condemned now that I don't care. All the religions are responsible for millions of women who became widows even while their husbands were alive; children who became orphans although their fathers were alive; old parents who became beggars because their young son on whom they were dependent had renounced the world. Nobody has counted how much harm the very idea of renunciation has done, and what is the gain? Just measure both, there seems to be no gain. All those who have renounced are simply dreaming about the same things, clinging in the same way, jealous in the same way.

I was in the Himalayas and I was just going to sit under a tree, when from another tree a monk, a Hindu monk, shouted, "Don't sit there. That belongs to my master."

I said, "My God, even here in this forest.... You have renounced the whole world, but you have not yet renounced the tree. And the tree belongs to nobody."

He said, "I am warning you, he is a dangerous man."

I said, "He has to be dangerous, because renunciation of the world can be done only by violent people."

How can you leave the world? This is your very sea, in which you are the fish. Leaving it you will die. How can a bird leave the sky? It is his very world. If he leaves the sky he will die. You cannot leave the world, but just on the margin you can take a few holidays, a few moments for yourself...and nobody will even know about it.

These small moments in which you drop the whole world as if it is a dream—and your own being remains the only reality—are the greatest moments of joy, peace, silence, blissfulness. These moments are divine. In these moments you are no more the ordinary human being, you have suddenly transcended humanness, you have transcended all form, you have entered into the formless existence. Your heart becomes the heartbeat of the whole existence.

This is the only practice possible, everything else is non-essential and dangerous. Be ordinary in every way, just keep a few small spaces here and there. The world goes on, you don't interfere in it, neither do you escape from it. You participate in it, and with participation you go on growing inside in these few moments. Remaining in the world and becoming a buddha, that is my message.

When someone has realized the great Law and the essence
of the Buddhas and patriarchs, we serve him, reverently
prostrating ourselves.

What can we do when somebody radiates consciousness, radiates the dance of existence? What do we have to offer? In the West people have always been concerned why people in the East touched the feet of their masters. They don't know it has become a traditional thing. Unfortunately everything becomes traditional; but basically, essentially, it has a great beauty. It is not a question of feet. It is simply a question of a gratitude which cannot be said, but only expressed by touching the feet of the master

Sakyamuni-buddha said: "When you meet a master who expounds
the supreme wisdom, do not consider his birth."

Don't ask what caste he belongs to, don't ask about his appearance. He may not look beautiful according to your ideas, he may not come from a high caste, from the Brahmins; he may be a sudra like Kabir or

DŌGEN

Dadu. He may not have renounced a kingdom like Buddha and Mahavira.

But everybody does not have a kingdom to renounce. I used to know a postmaster, a very poor man. He lived just nearby my house, so we used to talk once in a while. When his wife died—he had no children—he renounced the world. The same people who had never paid any attention to the poor man started touching his feet, and soon he became very famous. After twenty years I met him again through one of his disciples who said, "You should see him."

I said, "I know him."

But they said, "He has changed, he is a transformed man. He has renounced millions."

I said, "I know that in his post office account he had kept thirty-six rupees only. From where did he get millions?" But rumors...and he was enjoying those rumors. I said, "I am coming to put him in his right senses."

I asked him, "Please tell to your disciples how many rupees you had left in your post office account."

He looked so sadly at me. He said, "It will be better if we meet separately, alone, not with all these people."

I said, "I have to meet here in front of everybody, because these people think you have renounced millions. Now say clearly how many rupees!"

He said, "Thirty-six."

The disciples said, "Thirty-six? And you never told us before?"

He said, "I enjoyed the idea that I had renounced millions. And I never said anything...I simply did not deny it. So you cannot blame me."

And I said, "Tell these people the real thing."

He said, "What real thing?"

The real thing was that before he decided to renounce he asked me to write three speeches for him, one for ten minutes, one for twenty minutes, one for thirty minutes. He said, "I will memorize them completely and for a ten minute occasion I will use one; if twenty minutes are available I will use that one. I don't think more than thirty minutes will be available to me at conferences."

I said, "I am asking about those three speeches. Are you using them still or not?"

He said, "My God, you have come here to kill me completely! These people think I am a realized man!"

I said, "Tell these people that those three speeches were written by me."

He said, "I have to admit it." But he lost all his fame. Suddenly his disciples disappeared, everybody started laughing about the whole thing. But for twenty years continuously he had maintained his great learnedness with those three speeches.

I brought him back to my home. I said, "I need a gardener. You just do the garden and meditate with the plants, with the roses." And India has so many beautiful flowers, incomparable, because of the climate. The Indian rose has a fragrance that is not possible in a cold country; the fragrance is not released, it needs the sun. India has so many beautiful flowers, unknown to the world. I had a beautiful garden, so I put him to work.

He said, "I was enjoying being an enlightened one, and unfortunately somebody brought you there. In this old age now I have to become a gardener again."

I said, "This is far more authentic. Just be a gardener. It is a simple job. You can meditate and you can shower the water on the plants. The showering of water on the plants does not disturb your meditation. The flowers are not disturbing, the trees are very loving and very peaceful. I am giving you a really alive temple."

Dōgen is saying that when you meet a master don't think about his birth, don't bother about his appearance. All that is needed is a recognition that this is a man who has realized himself; everything else is non-essential. All that is needed now is a deep gratitude. It is a miracle to find such a man, and you have found him.

Your gratefulness will bring a spring to your being. The master's experience will start flowing towards you just as rivers flow down from the mountains towards the ocean. Your gratefulness becomes just like an ocean: vast, available. And the master's heights are like the mountains, from where the Ganges and thousands of other rivers come running, rushing, jumping from rock to rock, from valley to

valley, reaching towards the ocean. If you are with a master all that you need is a humbleness, a gratitude. And the master is bound to pour himself into you.

Dōgen continued, ...Both men and women can realize the Way. In any case, the realization of the Way should be respected, regardless of sex. This is an extremely excellent rule in the Way. Even a little girl of seven can become the teacher of the four classes of Buddhists...if she practices and realizes the Dhamma...We should make a venerative offering to her as if to the Buddhas.

Neither age matters nor birth matters, nor country nor race. What matters is your awareness, and awareness is neither Hindu nor Christian nor Mohammedan. It is just a fire, an eternal fire, invisible to the outside eye but visible when you close your eyes and go inward.

A haiku:

> *Mountains of green*
> *mountains of blue arise:*
> *My gratitude wells up*
> *and fills my eyes.*

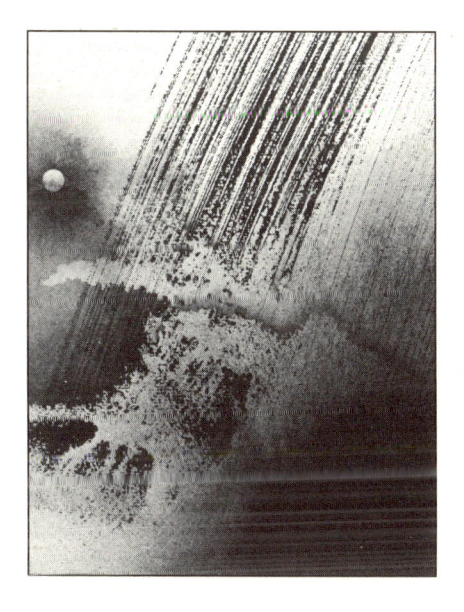

DIVE A LITTLE DEEP

Ryōkan wrote:

> *The thief*
> *left it behind—*
> *the moon at the window.*

This is just what Ryōkan wrote after the thief had gone. The whole story is beautiful. One night a thief entered into Ryōkan's small hut. Ryōkan had only one blanket which he used day and night to cover his body. That was his only possession. He was lying down but he was not asleep, so he opened his eyes and saw the thief entering. He felt great compassion for him because he knew there was nothing in the house. "If the poor fellow had informed me before, I could have begged something from the neighbors and kept it here for him to steal. But now what can I do?"

Seeing that there was nothing, that he had entered into a monk's hut, the thief started to go out. Ryōkan could not resist. He gave his blanket to the thief. The thief said, "What are you doing? You are standing naked. It is a very cold night!"

He said, "Don't be worried about me. But don't go empty-handed. I have enjoyed this moment, you have made me feel like a rich man. Thieves usually enter the palaces of emperors. By your entering here my hut has also become a palace, I have also become an emperor. In my joy this is just a gift."

Even the thief felt sorry for him and he said, "No, I cannot receive this gift because you don't have anything. How you are going to pass the night? It is so cold, and it is getting colder!"

Ryōkan said with tears in his eyes, "You remind me again and again of my poverty. If it was in my power I would have taken hold of the full moon and given it to you."

When the thief left he wrote in his diary:
The thief
left it behind—
the moon at the window.

These haikus are not ordinary poems. These are statements of deep meditativeness.

DŌGEN

Maneesha has asked:

Our Beloved Master,
What is the essence of our Master's Law?

Maneesha, here I am not—just an empty space, a hollow bamboo. If you want to join with me, nothing else is needed. Just be utterly empty and silent. This is your master's dhamma. And in fact, this is all the masters' dhamma. Become a hollow bamboo so that you can be turned into a flute and songs of immense beauty can pass through you. They will not be your songs, they will be songs of existence.

Before we enter into today's meditation...the bamboos are very silent and waiting for your laughter. My gardeners have informed me that they have never seen bamboos growing so fast. Particularly as the evening arrives they all start jumping up. They are participants, they meditate with you. They cannot say anything, but saying does not matter. They understand your laughter certainly.

Bruno Meatball, a truck driver, is trying to change a flat tire by the side of the road. He is hammering away with all his might, cursing and swearing with each unsuccessful blow.

The village priest is passing by and decides to help him. He sits down by Bruno's side and says to him, "I will pray to God; all miracles are possible." He then gives Bruno a little lecture about offering a prayer instead of curses when confronted with trouble.

Finally "The Meatball" says that he is willing to try anything, just to get the tire off the wheel. So they both kneel beside the truck and pray.

When Bruno goes back to work he gives the tire one blow, and it almost jumps off by itself.

The priest looks on in amazement, and cries, "Well, I'll be fucked!"

Mr. and Mrs. Polite live in a nice big house in Propertown, U.S.A. And they are really polite. When Mrs. Polite brings Mr. Polite his dinner, he says, "Thank you so much, darling."

And Mrs. Polite says, "Oh you are so welcome, sweetheart. Actually, I should thank you for being such a lovely husband to serve."

Then Mr. Polite says, "No, I should doubly thank you for being such a lovely wife...." And so on.

Anyway, they are all so polite that one evening Mr. Polite sees a lonely middle-aged fellow standing in the rain. Politely, he invites the stranger into the house for a nice, hearty meal. Two hours later, Mr. Polite stumbles across the stranger making love in the hallway to their lovely daughter, Pussy Polite.

Upon seeing this, Mr. Polite says, very politely, "Pussy, dear, where are your manners? Arch your back and help the gentleman to get his balls off this cold marble floor!"

After many attempts, Gilbert Goldditch finally manages to get Gorgeous Gloria to go to his apartment with him. After a few drinks, Gilbert puts on some soft music, and they settle down on the sofa.

A few minutes later Gloria says, "You know, Gilbert, you are the first man I have met whose kisses make me sit up and open my eyes."

"Really?" says Gilbert, happily.

"Yes," replies Gloria. "Usually they have the opposite effect!"

Mikhail Gorbachev gets up in the morning and goes out onto his balcony to get some fresh air. The sun is rising. "Good morning, red sun!" he exclaims.

"Long live Mikhail Gorbachev!" the sun replies.

Very happy with this, Gorbachev goes about his business. After a busy morning he goes out onto his balcony again, and sees the sun at its height.

"Good afternoon, sun!" he shouts out.

"Long live Comrade Gorbachev, General Secretary of the Communist Party of the Soviet Union!" replies the sun.

Very pleased, Gorbachev returns to his work.

That evening, after a hard day, he comes out once again onto his favorite balcony. He sees the sun setting, and with a smile cries out, "Good evening, my little sun!"

"I am in the West now," replies the sun, "so fuck you!"

DŌGEN

Now, Nivedano, give the beat…

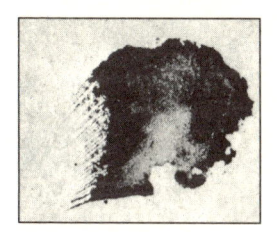

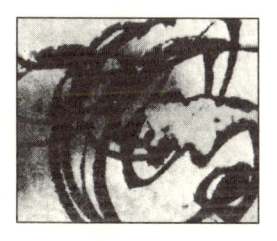

Nivedano…

Be silent.
Close your eyes.
Feel your body to be frozen,
and just go in…deeper and deeper.
At the deepest is your immortal self.
Don't be afraid of the unknown,
rush towards the center like an arrow.
Just don't stop on the periphery,
because only at the center,
where nothing moves,
you are a buddha.

DIVE A LITTLE DEEP

To make it more clear, Nivedano

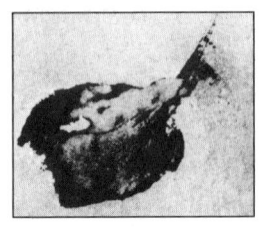

Relax,
let go, forget the body,
forget the mind,
just remember that you are
pure consciousness, just an awareness.
And without going a single step anywhere
you have arrived home.

Nivedano...

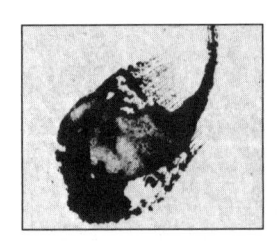

Come back,
but come back as buddhas
and sit down for a few moments...
remembering, rejoicing, making a contact...
that in your every activity
this consciousness
will always be like an undercurrent.
Once this experience of buddhahood
becomes a solid experience,
it expresses in all your activities—
in your words, in your silences,
in your days, in your nights.

It becomes your constant companion.
Ultimately
you deserve the final disappearance
and only the buddha remains.
A pure awareness
is the most beautiful lotus
that has ever blossomed.

Okay, Maneesha?
Yes, Beloved Master.

Can we celebrate the ten thousand buddhas?
Yes, Beloved Master.

THE MOON
NEVER BREAKS THE WATER

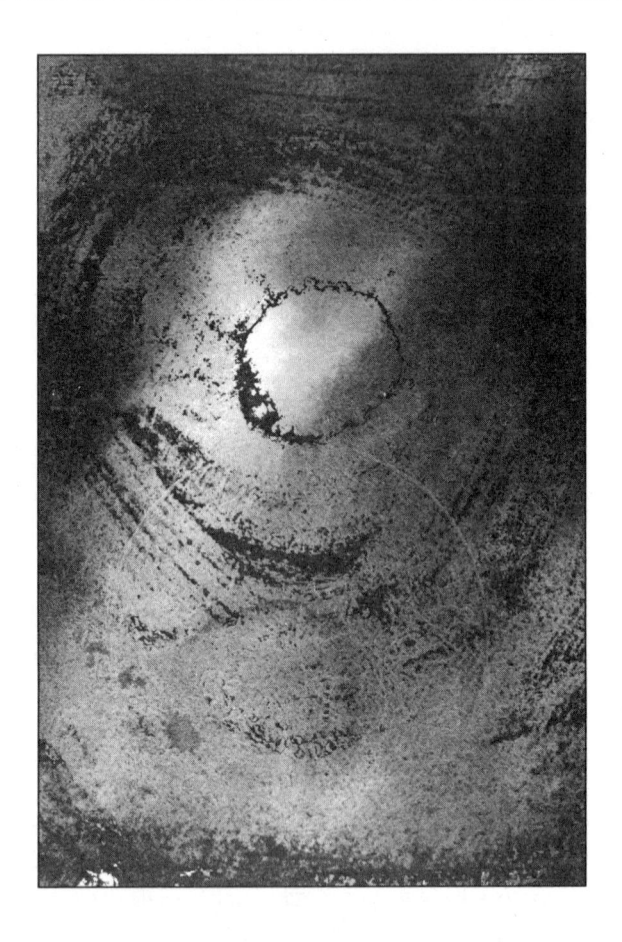

The sun rises within you
and the moon hangs within you,
and the stars are part of your inner sky.

*Our Beloved Master,
Dōgen wrote:*
When we achieve enlightenment, it is just like the moon reflecting itself on the water. The moon will not get wet, nor is the water broken. The moonlight, however vast, reflects itself on a small quantity of water. The whole moon and the whole sky both reflect themselves even in a dewdrop on the grass, or in a drop of water.

As the moon never breaks the water, so enlightenment never destroys the man. As the dewdrop never obstructs the reflection of the moon, so a man never obstructs the coming of enlightenment. The deeper the moon reflects itself in the water, the higher the moon is. We should realize that the long and short of time are quite one with the large and small of water, and the broad and narrow of the moon.

Maneesha, Dōgen is making a very specific point. It deserves absolute attention and concern, because he is saying nobody obstructs your enlightenment. Then why are you not enlightened?

Nobody in the whole existence is interested in becoming an obstacle to you. It is something of major significance that has to be understood.

As we go along in the sutra, I would like to make it clear to you what it is that is obstructing. Certainly you are not obstructing it. And existence loves it, rejoices in it. The whole universe dances in every man's enlightenment. One part of it, which had been groping in the dark, has come back home in its full glory. The whole existence receives him with a showering of flowers. So there is no question of any obstruction from existence. And there is no question about yourself. Then who is obstructing? There certainly are obstructions; otherwise there would be no need to become enlightened—you would be enlightened. There would be no need for any master to tell you. It is a little bit complicated, but not so complicated that you cannot understand and overcome it. Dōgen says:

When we achieve enlightenment, it is just like the moon reflecting itself on the water...
So peaceful, so silent. The moon reflects on the surface of the water. In fact, nothing is happening. The moon is in its own place, it has not moved even a little inch towards the water; nor is the water disturbed even a little bit.

But in a silent lake the moon's reflection becomes even more beautiful than the moon itself, because the lake also adds some beauty to it. It makes it more alive and more fragile.

Enlightenment—according to Dōgen, and I agree with him absolutely—*is just like the moon reflecting itself on the water.* There is no effort on the part of the water, that the moon has to be reflected. There is no commandment that has to be followed, no doctrines that have to be practiced, no yoga postures...so that the moon can reflect itself in the water. There is not even a desire, not even a longing... not even a faint longing. And the same is the situation on the part of the moon—the moon has no desire to be reflected. Both are desireless, but the reflection happens on its own accord. So does enlightenment. Just in a silent, peaceful consciousness it suddenly reflects your buddhahood.

But the lake has to be silent. If there are too many ripples or too many waves on the lake the reflection will be broken. The reflection may be broken in many parts and you will not be able to see the moon, but only a silver line spread all over the lake. It will not be a true reflection; it will not be representative of the moon. The lake, when silent and still, doing nothing...not even any waves...and the moon reflects.

Your consciousness has its own way of making waves, ripples. What are your thoughts except ripples on a lake? What are your emotions, your moods, your sentiments? What is your whole mind?—just a turmoil. And because of this turmoil you cannot see your own nature. You go on missing yourself. You meet everybody in the world and you never meet yourself.

The moon will not get wet...

Obviously, there is no question of the moon getting wet because it is reflected in the lake.

...nor is the water broken—by the moon.

The moon is not like a stone that has been thrown in the water, it is just a reflection. When you stand before a mirror you don't disturb the mirror. You come and go; the mirror remains exactly in its position, undisturbed.

The moonlight, however vast, reflects itself on a small quantity of water. The whole moon and the whole sky both reflect themselves even in a dewdrop, on the grass, or in a drop of water.
As the moon never breaks the water, so enlightenment never destroys the man.

This is a very great statement. It does not destroy the man but it destroys the shadow of the man, with which you are identified. It takes away all that is false and leaves behind only the real, the authentic, the honest.

As the dewdrop never obstructs the reflection of the moon, so a man never obstructs the coming of enlightenment. The deeper the moon reflects itself in the water, the higher the moon is. We should realize that the long and short of time are quite one with the large and small of water, and the broad and narrow of the moon.

What is your shadow that is obstructing your reality? Your shadow

has to be understood perfectly well: it is your personality. It is what you have been proposed to be, it is what you have been brought up to be. It is all those voices of your mothers and fathers, your teachers. They make your personality; they create a pseudo-ness around you. Your knowledge...nobody ever asked whether it is yours.

I have been expelled from many colleges. The principals would call me in and tell me, "You cannot harass my professor."

I said, "Your professor has made some statements, and I have simply asked him, 'Is it your own experience?' Do you call that harassing? Do you want to expel *me,* or should you expel a man who is teaching something which is not his own experience?"

I would tell the principals, "Call that teacher who has reported against me. He has to confront me. I don't care about any examination or any degree, and I don't care about your college. But things have to be put right."

Even the principals would say to me, "You are right, but you don't understand our problem. We are all carrying borrowed knowledge. We don't know exactly what the truth is, but we are talking about it. You are a nuisance. Nobody else is asking such questions. Now this professor—who has even threatened to resign if you are not expelled immediately from the college—is an old, very senior man. He is almost near his retirement, and he has never been violent or angry. There has been nothing against him during his twenty years' service in the college. And suddenly you have made him almost insane. He has not come for three days, he has closed his doors, he does not want to speak to anybody from the college, he does not answer the phone. He has simply written a note, 'Unless you expel that student, I am not going to come to the college.'"

I said, "There is no problem. You can expel your whole college, you need not be worried about that. But I will follow that man—college or no college. I know his home. I may not be a student in your college, that does not mean... Where is he going to live? I will knock on his doors. Either he has to recognize the fact that his knowledge is borrowed or he has to speak honestly from his experience. I simply want to provoke him."

I was surprised to know that great professors...because I have

been in many colleges, it was a great opportunity. Usually, one ends up with just one college. I was being expelled from one college to another, and later from one university to another. The second university accepted me with the condition that I would not trouble the professors.

I said, "What kind of poverty is this? If you don't know the answer you can simply say, 'I don't know.' But that hurts your ego."

They asked me to write down that they are accepting me on the condition that I will not attend any classes. Strange! I don't think this has happened to anybody else in the whole world. "If I am not to attend the classes, then why are you admitting me? And how am I going to manage my percentage of attendance so I can appear for the examination?"

The vice-chancellor said, "I will take care of your percentage. You are present—one hundred percent! That is my promise to you. But please, don't go to any class, because I have heard about you so much from other professors, principals. The other vice-chancellor who has expelled you phoned me, 'Beware of this boy.' I am accepting you because I can see the point that you are not wrong; just our whole system is wrong. Your only fault is that you are pointing to our wound. I can understand you; that's why I am giving you admission.

"But the professors will not be able to understand. You are so accurate in hitting at the weakest point that these ordinary professors …after all they are just working for money; there is no question of truth or good or beauty. They are not concerned about these things; they are concerned with their salaries, they are concerned with their position. It is politics: the lecturer wants to be the reader, the reader wants to be the professor, the professor wants to be the head of the department, the head of the department wants to be the dean of the faculty, the dean wants to be the vice-chancellor—nobody is interested in what you are asking. So your presence has created a fear."

I had to accept this, but as I signed the agreement and he signed my admittance, I told him, "I can at least meet the professors on the road, I can knock on their doors. The promise is only for the classes. I can go to the library—these things are not included."

He said, "This is difficult."

And I used to do that—knock on professors' doors. And they would say, "Just leave us at peace. We are tired. The questions that you ask are unanswerable. We don't know, we are not seekers; we are just educators. We have learned from others who have learned from others. We don't know what we are teaching, whether it is true or whether we are simply repeating superstitions." I would catch hold of them in the library.

And the vice-chancellor told me, "Look, you stop professors on the road when they are coming to their classes, and you ask them, 'Please answer this question before you enter the class, because I cannot enter the classroom.' It is not part of our agreement, so I cannot insist on it, but don't harass."

I said, "But I can stand outside the classroom and from the window I will shout the question. So it is better if we settle it here. I will never enter the classroom, but the rest is not part of the agreement." The vice-chancellor had forgotten that every classroom had a window. "I can stand outside in the fresh air rather than in the rotten inside air and I can ask anything that I want.

"And you should understand it clearly, that if I ask a question and the professor doesn't answer it, then the whole class will ask the same question. What you request is not part of the agreement."

I used to distribute my question to all the class, "If he does not answer me, one by one you stand up and ask the question…until he is finished!"

But who is preventing all these people who are knowledgeable from seeing that their very knowledge is the barrier?

Dōgen is right that enlightenment is your natural being, as natural as the moon reflecting on the silent lake. No effort on any side, no desire on any side…it is a happening. But you have not been left a clean, silent lake. So much rubbish—in the name of religion, in the name of politics, in the name of society—has been imposed on you: that is what is making the barrier. And the poor moon cannot reflect on you. You have to destroy this whole wall that is preventing you from looking at things as they are—not as you have been told. You have to get rid of all ideology that has been implanted in you, all your conditioning.

Even very intelligent people I have seen behave so superstitiously —you cannot believe. There are countries where the number thirteen is thought to be a dangerous number. Perhaps somebody died or committed suicide on the thirteenth some time back; perhaps somebody jumped from the thirteenth floor of a hotel, and now people have become certain it is bad luck. There are hotels which don't have a room number thirteen; after twelve it jumps to fourteen. They don't have a thirteenth floor; after the twelfth just comes the fourteenth. It is the thirteenth, but the hotel does not recognize it as the thirteenth.

People don't get married on the thirteenth, out of fear that life will be a misery; and they don't look around to see that whether you marry on the thirteenth or the fourteenth or the fifteenth, marriage *is* going to be a misery. Don't blame the dates, and don't blame the days. Marriage itself is a desire to be miserable, a deep down desire...a partnership in misery. "You look so beautiful" means, "You look so miserable. I am also very miserable...let's be together"—as if by being together the misery will disappear. But it will not disappear, it will not only be doubled, it will be increased by much more than double.

The whole world knows it, but we go on with our conditioning. If you are unmarried every married person you know is very sorry for you, "Poor fellow, he has remained a bachelor; he does not know the happiness of misery."

When I came back from the university, naturally my parents were concerned that I should get married. But they were afraid to even ask me because they knew that once I say no, then it is forever. Then there is no way to drag me into saying yes. They knew me perfectly well, that it was absolutely improbable that I would say yes. So how to ask? That was their problem.

I told them, "It seems everybody wants to ask me something, and I am ready. So why you don't ask it? You whisper with each other."

Finally my father found a friend, a supreme court advocate, a very successful man in his profession. He asked him, "We are not in a position even to ask. Now you have to do something."

He said, "Don't be worried. The whole country knows that when I take a case in my hand..."

My father said, "This is not the supreme court, and this is no ordinary case. I warn you—if any trouble arises for you, I will not be responsible."

He said, "What trouble? I am coming this weekend and I will talk to your son, and I will take care of it. It is a question of argumentation."

My father said, "You don't know him, but come. We will all enjoy it."

So everybody was ready. He came. I touched his feet because he was my father's friend, and I was as respectful as always. I said to him, "Before the debate starts..."

He said, "What debate?"

I said, "You know it, I know it, and everybody else present here knows it. But before it starts, I want you honestly to answer one question: Are you satisfied in your marriage? I have informed your wife, and if you say anything wrong...she is just sitting in the other room."

He said, "What? She is here? My God, I don't want to be entangled in this affair."

I said, "It has not even started."

He said, "I don't want to take the case."

I said, "This is not the court. You have come with such a wide chest, and now you have suddenly become a rat. I will have to wash my hands...I touched your feet."

It was only a fiction, I had not asked his wife. But I knew that she used to beat him.

He said, "Your father asked me."

I said, "I am perfectly ready. If you can convince me that marriage is the right way of living, I will get married. But if you fail in convincing me you will have to divorce."

He said, "My God, your father was right that this would be a difficult case. I simply withdraw! I don't want to say a single word. Let me think. Next week I will come."

He never came. But every week I would go to his home and his wife would ask me, "What is the matter? Whenever you come he hides himself in the bathroom. I knock on the bathroom door and he

says, 'No, I cannot come out right now. Tell him to leave me alone. I have become so afraid of him I cannot go to the market, because—who knows?—he may stop me in the street and start the debate. And I cannot afford...'"

So the wife said to me, "But what is the matter? Why is he so afraid?"

I shouted to the lawyer, "Either you come out, or I am going to tell your wife."

He immediately came out. He said, "Just forgive me. For God's sake, just drop the matter. I will never mention the subject to you or anybody..."

The wife said, "But what is the matter that you are so much afraid? You perspire and it is air conditioned. You hide and you tell me to lie that you are not at home. And he is such a stubborn person, he keeps on coming."

I said, "This is the problem, you have to be the judge. This man, your husband, wants me to get married. What is your opinion?"

She said, "Married? If you want to be miserable, get married. Just look at this man. I have been reforming him since the day we married. I have almost finished him. He fights in the supreme court like a lion, and in the house he is just a stray dog. Even the children understand it. Even the children blackmail him, 'You give us five rupees, otherwise we will tell mother.' And he cannot even ask what it is that they will tell; but it's enough that he has been talking to the neighbor's wife so sweetly." Because then the wife would be really dangerous, she would beat him. Now the poor fellow is dead.

I told my parents and my family, "Don't bring others unnecessarily, because I am fundamentally against marriage. There is no question of my marrying, it is something fundamental to me that marriage is a wrong conception."

Two persons can be in love and live together and the moment their love disappears—as everything disappears in this world—they should depart with gratitude to each other, with friendship, with pleasant memories of the past days. Marriage is absolutely unnatural. That's why you don't see any animals in the psychiatric hospitals. You don't see them lying on the psychoanalyst's couch, they don't go mad.

THE MOON NEVER BREAKS THE WATER

Man has had so many layers imposed on him about everything; he thinks all these thoughts are his own. As a seeker you have to discriminate very carefully between what is yours and what has been given to you. And the moment you start sorting it out, you will be amazed to know that you don't have anything of your own. You are just a silent lake. And in that silent lake your buddhahood arises. Your nature *is*, in its purity, in its splendor, in its blissfulness.

And nobody is trying to prevent you from becoming enlightened. Those people—those teachers, those parents—they were not aware; they were as unconscious.... They were also victims of their parents, of their teachers, of their rabbis and their pundits and their shankaracharyas and their popes. They were victims, and they have given to you as your heritage all their suffering and all their misery. Now you have to put all that load aside. Buddhahood is your natural self. Just put aside everything that is not arising within you, flowering within you.

In a way, in the beginning you will feel poor. All your knowledge is gone, all your superstitions are gone, your religions are gone, your political ideologies are gone—you will feel very poor. But this poverty is of tremendous value, because only in this poverty arises your natural richness, your natural flowers, your natural ecstasies. The natural man is not destroyed by enlightenment. But you are not natural, you are polluted.

And everybody is harming everybody else by creating these conditions. In a better society children will not be taught any religion, any politics. They will be taught how to think, how to doubt; not how to believe. They will be taught to be more intelligent, to be more reflective. And the whole world will be full of enlightened people.

Enlightenment is just your naturalness. This is the great contribution of Zen. All other religions are belief systems, Zen is not. All other religions will ask you to believe in God, in heaven, in hell. All other religions will have a thousand and one beliefs. Zen has no belief system. Its whole effort is to discover your natural self, which is covered with the dust of all kinds of good intentions, of beautiful thoughts, of great beliefs. All that dust has to be cleaned off. And then you are left alone in your naturalness.

DŌGEN

A haiku of Hoitsu:

> *Buddha:*
> *cherry flowers*
> *in moonlight.*

Just so simple. Just so beautiful.
Buddha:
cherry flowers
in moonlight.

Ryōta wrote:

So brilliant a moonshine:
if ever I am born again—
a hilltop pine!

He is asking that if he is going to be born again, he would like to be a hilltop pine. Such a beautiful moon, hanging over the hilltop pine...

These people are not ordinary poets. They are expressing an authentic longing to be natural, peaceful, silent...*a hilltop pine!*... because man seems to be so insane.

Another Zen poet:

> *Searching for Him*
> *Took my strength*
> *One night I bent*
> *my pointing finger—*
> *Never such a moon!*

These people are natural poets. They have dropped all ideologies. They have started having relationships with pine trees and the clouds and the lightning; with the hills, with the rivers, with the ocean. They have dropped out of the human world which is absolutely false and they have regained again their roots in nature.

This is, in my vision, the only religion in the world worth calling religion. All other religions are just exploitations of man and his search for himself. They are deviations, distractions. They lead you away from yourself, they don't bring you home.

Maneesha has asked:

Our Beloved Master,
Dōgen seems to be saying that the more profoundly enlightenment touches one's being, the more potent is the enlightenment. Is it true that there are no grades of enlightenment—that one is either enlightened or not—but that enlightenment, like wine, becomes more and more mature?

Maneesha, your understanding is right. There are no grades of enlightenment—either you are enlightened or not enlightened. But certainly, as enlightenment deepens, matures, reaches to your very roots... It is just the right symbol: like wine, the older it is the better.

There are wine collectors... You can find fifty-year-old wine, one-hundred-year-old wine—they are all wines. Fresh wine just produced from the garden is also wine. But a hundred-year-old wine has

attained a certain quality of intensity, a density, which is lacking in the new arrivals. There are experts in the world who can tell exactly, just by taking a sip, how old is the wine.

It happened in a pub that a man said to the bartender, "Here is one hundred dollars. If you are ready to gamble with me, I will taste any wine you want me to taste and I will tell you its exact year." It was unbelievable, because wine testing is a very fine art. The offer was accepted. Each time he tells the right year when the wine was made, the bartender will pay him one hundred dollars.

He went on tasting and telling the exact year. It was so amazing, all the drinkers and drunkards who were there sitting on different benches gathered around; even those who were completely drunk became awake, "What is happening?" And the man was amazing.

Then suddenly a man from the back said, "I also want to join in the contest because I have got a wine. If you can tell me..."

So he brought a full cup. The man tasted it, spat it out, and he said, "You idiot. This is human urine!"

But the man said, "Whose? I know it is human urine—but whose? Unless you can tell me whose, you are not a great taster."

Enlightenment certainly has no grades, but as time passes it deepens, sharpens, matures, becomes more and more rich.

Before we enter into our daily meditation... The bamboos are so silent, just waiting for your laughter. And remember one thing, when you laugh, don't just laugh for conformity.

Secondly, when you laugh, laugh totally, without any considerations. Don't hold anything back. Learn to laugh from Sardar Gurudayal Singh, who is a laugh unto himself—a real joke. He is the only man in the whole world I have come across who laughs before the joke. There are people who laugh in the middle of the joke because they suddenly realize what is going to happen. But from the very beginning, when I have not even started...that is the real and authentic man of laughter. And I know...he has his disciples. He is a very respected, old sannyasin. People sit around him just to have a good laugh.

Joe Speak-Easy, the successful lawyer, is married to a woman who nags him constantly. She nags him about his appearance, about how much he drinks, about how little he loves her—about almost everything. So Joe starts staying later at his office to avoid her.

One day, after weeks of defending a client called William Wright who is on trial for murder, Joe comes home very depressed. He has lost the case, and Wright is to be executed that night unless the governor pardons him.

As Joe enters the house, his wife begins, "Where have you been? It's after ten o'clock."

"Ah, nag, nag, nag," he says in disgust, and goes to pour himself a drink.

"The minute you come home," snaps his wife, "you start drinking. Not even a hello for me!"

"Ah, nag, nag, nag," sighs Joe. Then he goes upstairs for a bath, telling his wife that he is expecting a phone call from the governor.

While he is in the bath, the call comes—Wright has been pardoned. Joe's wife decides to tell him the good news herself. As she enters the bathroom Joe is standing naked, bending over the tub.

"Hey, Joe," says his wife. "They are not hanging Wright tonight."

Joe snaps back, "Ah, nag, nag, nag!"

Old Zeb, the back-woods Virginia farmer, has been screwing one of his favorite pigs for years. Suddenly, Zeb is hit by pangs of guilt and conscience that torture him so much he decides to go and tell the priest about it in confession. Father Fungus is shocked and he really does not know how to handle this one.

"Well," says the priest to old Zeb, "tell me, is the pig male or female?"

"She's female, of course," snorts Zeb. "What do you think I am—some kind of a pervert?"

Pope the Polack is sitting on the train next to Ronald Reagan on their way back to Washington from Killjews, Alabama. The pope strikes up a conversation with two big black guys, Rufus and Leroy, in the compartment.

"Hello, gentleman," says the pope. "Where are you going?"

"D.C." says Rufus.

"What did he say?" asks the slightly deaf president.

"He says they are going to Washington, D.C.—just like us," says the pope. "Tell me," the Polack continues, "what brings you all the way up to Washington?"

"We know a real far-out chick up there," smiles Leroy.

"What did he say?" asks the hard-of-hearing Ronnie.

"He says they have a girlfriend up there," shouts back the pope to the president. Then turning to the black guys, Pope the Polack says, "She must be quite a girl for you to go all this way to see her."

"Man, I'll say," smiles Rufus.

"Sure," says Leroy. "She's a real cool bitch. She wears black boots with spurs, carries a whip and indulges in every delight known to man!"

"What did he say?" shouts the deaf president.

Pope the Polack turns to Ronnie and screams, "He says they know Nancy!"

Now...Nivedano...

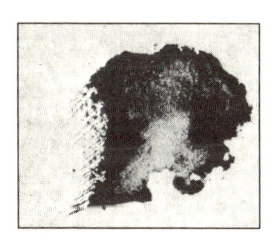

Nivedano...

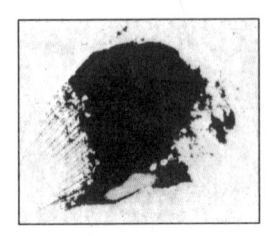

Be silent...close your eyes...
no movement of the body.
Gather your consciousness inwards.
Deeper...and deeper...
just like an arrow
cutting all the layers of garbage.
Enter into your center.
In this moment of silence,
in this moment of innocence,
you are no more your shadow.
You are yourself.
This being yourself is called
"the arising of the moon,"
or "arising of the buddha."
Each one in his nature is the buddha...
the enlightened one, the awakened one.
Every man is just a seed...
he only needs to find the right soil
in which to disappear, disperse his personality,
his knowledge, his mind...
And suddenly the moon
is reflected in the lake.
And suddenly the pine on the hilltop
touching the moon.
And suddenly out of nowhere
arises your buddhahood.
Remember this—twenty-four hours—
not as a thought,

but as a heartache,
so that it becomes an undercurrent.
Whatever you are doing
becomes different because you are different.
Your touch has a grace now;
your smile has a sincerity;
your eyes become just silent lakes.
Your action reflects your heart,
your being, your joy, your dance.
There is no other god.
There is no other temple.
Except you—awakened to your full glory,
to your full splendor—
there is no religion.

To make this point more clear, Nivedano...

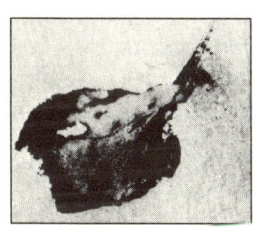

Relax...let go...
just die...
to the body, to the mind,
to everything of this world.
What remains is just a pure sky,
utterly blissful, immensely ecstatic.
This is your forgotten language.
Only this kind of silence,
a deepening into yourself,
can connect you with existence.
And being connected with the existence,
the whole life becomes a festival,
a ceremony.

Not only life,
but death also, because there is no death.
There is only life
and life and life,
and higher peaks and deeper valleys.
From beginningless to endless existence,
you are spread.
Everything is somehow within you.
The sun rises within you
and the moon hangs within you,
and the stars are part of your inner sky.
Remember that the inner sky
is vaster than the outer.
Blessed are those
who have tasted this inner juice
of pure existence.

Nivedano...

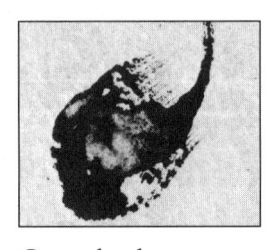

Come back...
but don't leave the experience behind.
Sit down and collect the experience—
the joy of it, the benediction of it.
And remember not to forget.
It has to become a constant breathing,
a heartbeat.
Only then you will feel fulfilled.
Only then you will feel you are not meaningless.
Only then your life is a grandeur.
This grandeur is already there,

just you have to discover it.
Just a few layers of dust—
remove them.
We meditate every evening
simply so that you go on deepening
more and more,
so that the wine becomes older and older.
So that your buddhahood
becomes an absolute certainty.
It is not an argument,
it is an experience.

Okay, Maneesha?
Yes, Beloved Master.

Can we celebrate the ten thousand buddhas and their gathering here?
Yes, Beloved Master.

THE SKY IS NOT SCRATCHED BY THE CLOUD

A cloud,
trying to enwrap the moonbeams,
a monsoon shower.

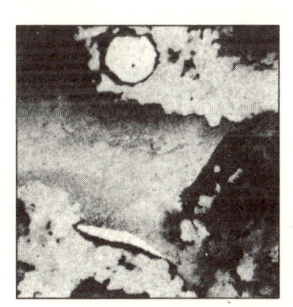

*Our Beloved Master,
Dōgen said,*
*The Buddha said, If you want to understand the true meaning of
the Buddha-nature, you should correctly understand its momentary
manifestations.*

When the right time comes, the Buddha-nature will manifest itself.
Dōgen continued:
*Many monks, both past and present, have believed that the phrase,
"When the right time comes," means to wait for the Buddha-nature to
manifest itself in the future. They think that if they continue training in
the Way, the Buddha-nature will naturally manifest itself at the right
time. Until that time comes, they mistakenly conclude that the Buddha-
nature will not manifest itself, even should they visit a master in search of
the Dharma or train diligently.*

*Based on this false conclusion, they meaninglessly return to the
ordinary world and vainly wait for the right time to come.*

The words, "When the right time comes," means that the right time has

THE SKY IS NOT SCRATCHED BY THE CLOUD

already come. There can be no doubt about this. Even should doubts arise, they are nothing but the manifestation of the Buddha-nature in ourselves. "The right time" means that we should make the most of every day.

If the right time were something which came, the Buddha-nature would not come.

This is because the right time has already come; the Buddha-nature has already manifested itself. This fact is quite clear, for there has never been a right time that has not come, nor a Buddha-nature which has not manifested itself.

Maneesha, man is by birth a buddha—every man, good or bad, right or wrong, sinner or saint, it does not matter. As far as one's buddhahood is concerned, it remains untouched by what you do, by what is your behavior. Because this is the case, the problem arises that if everybody is a buddha then why this effort and endeavor, this seeking and searching for buddhahood?

This question was asked not only to Dōgen, it was also asked to Gautam Buddha himself, who is only one buddha in the long line of buddhas who have passed before him and after him; but perhaps the most prominent, perhaps the most recognized. To satisfy the ordinary questioner Buddha said, "It will come in its own time," just as flowers come in their own time and clouds come in their own time and the sun rises in its own time.

In existence there is a continuity of timing. It is not that today the moon will be a little late or the sun will continue a little longer. There is absolute certainty that everything happens in nature when the right time comes, so the right time simply means the right opportunity, the right climate, the right readiness, receptivity. And then you need not be worried about buddhahood, because as far as buddhahood is concerned you already have it. What is missing is a recognition. You have forgotten your name, that is all that is missing. Perhaps a certain situation is needed in which you can be reminded about your name.

Before I talk about Dōgen's sutra I would love to share with you

an incident in Edison's life. He was such a prominent scientist, such a great teacher, that nobody ever referred to him by name. His parents died early and he was so involved in his work that he had no friends. All that he had were scientists who were studying under him. Obviously they could not call him by his name, Edison. They all called him 'Professor'.

Slowly slowly he himself forgot what his name was. If for fifty years nobody uses your name and then suddenly somebody calls you by your name, it is possible you will get a shock. You will feel that somehow you remember this fellow...a memory, a faraway echo in the mountains. But ordinarily this does not happen because every day you are reminded of your name.

It was a special case with Edison. His parents died early, and he was a genius from his very childhood. He alone was capable of inventing one thousand things which had never existed in the world. You will not be able to find anything around you on which there is not Edison's signature.

In the first world war the ration card was for the first time introduced, and everybody had to go to the office to register. Obviously every office where names were registered was crowded, people were standing in queues. Edison also stood in a queue. When the man standing ahead of him gave all the information and got his ration card and went away, the clerk looking at the list called the name loudly, "Will Mr. Edison come up now?" And Edison looked here and there. He could not remember...there was a certain memory that he used to know a fellow of the name Edison, but not for fifty years had anybody called him by his name.

A man in the queue recognized that the fellow standing in front was the famous Edison, and he was looking here and there. The man said, "The one you are looking for, you *are*. Have you forgotten your name, Professor?"

He said, "My God, it is good that you reminded me, otherwise I would have lost my ration card. I was trying hard to remember; the name seems to be familiar, but I could not connect it with myself. For fifty years people have been calling me 'Professor', 'Doctor', but nobody has...because I don't have any friends, I don't have my parents."

THE SKY IS NOT SCRATCHED BY THE CLOUD

Buddhahood is nothing but another name of your basic nature, your essential nature. And nobody has ever pointed it out to you. On the contrary, everybody has been sticking names, degrees...creating a personality around you, and slowly slowly you start accepting it. If everybody is saying that you are intelligent, very intelligent, you start believing it.

We are all victims of a crowd. One of my professors, S.S. Roy, did not agree with me. He said, "It is impossible to forget one's own name. This story of Edison must be your creation."

I said, "Please give me some time to prove it."

He said, "What can you prove?"

I said, "You just wait." And after two, three days, when things were forgotten, I went to his house, told his wife... Rajendra Anuragi here knows professor S.S. Roy—he was also a student in the same university at that time. I told his wife, "When Professor Roy wakes up in the morning you just do a little kindness for me."

She said, "Whatever you want...what do you want?"

I said, "It is very small. You just ask him, 'Why are you looking so pale? Have you been suffering from fever? Could you not sleep well? Is something bothering you? Are you having a headache?' And whatever he says, just note it down exactly in his own words, and I will collect that note later on."

She said, "I don't understand what you are doing."

I said, "It is just an experiment. Later on I will explain to you, but right now don't ask more than that."

Then I told his gardener, "When he comes out, you ask him, 'What happened to you? You are looking so sick, and where are you going? Just go in and rest, and I will call the doctor.'"

And the gardener said, "But what is the purpose of all this? He is perfectly healthy!"

I said, "That is not the point. I will explain the whole thing to you later. Whatever he says, keep this card with you, write it down exactly in his own words."

And this I did from his house up to the philosophy department. The postmaster used to live in between, and another professor—I told them, "Just be kind enough to participate in an experiment."

And the final person was the peon of the philosophy department. I told him, "You don't bother, you just..."—he was a strong and big man—"you just take hold of Professor Roy as he enters, and whether he struggles or not, you lie him down on the sofa."

He said, "What are you saying? I will be kicked out from my service!"

I said, "Nobody can kick you out. I make the guarantee."

But he said, "This is a strange kind of experiment. Is it an experiment on me or on Professor Roy? I have children and a wife and old parents, and I am a poor man. Don't disturb my job."

I said, "It is nothing to do with you. You simply do it."

He said, "Okay, if you say so." He knew that I was so much loved by Professor Roy. He said, "If you are saying, I will do it, just because of you."

And I said, "Take this card. Whatever he says, write it down, and I will collect it just within a few minutes."

I followed Roy from his house. As he was moving onwards I started collecting the notes. To the wife he said, "What? I am perfectly healthy. I have slept well. Who said to you that my face is looking pale?"

She said, "There is no need for anybody to say, I can see you are looking pale."

He said, "All nonsense. Just female rubbish!"

But a doubt arose in him. As he was getting ready to go to the university the gardener took his hand and told him, "What are you doing? You cannot even walk rightly, you are wobbly! Just go in and rest. I will go and call the doctor."

And to him he said, "Yes, I think I need some rest. The whole night it seems I have not rested, and a little fever also seems to be there, but it is not too much. At least I can go up to the university, tell the head of the department and come back."

And the postmaster who was his great friend, he looked so much afraid, and said, "No, I will not let you go alone. I'm coming with you."

He said, "I'm really sick. I am feeling very weak. It is very kind of you to offer."

The postmaster said, "You can take my car."

THE SKY IS NOT SCRATCHED BY THE CLOUD

He said, "No, there is no need to take your car, I will manage. But if I need your car I will phone from the office. But I am feeling a kind of trembling, strange. In my whole life I have never felt such a trembling."

All these notes I was collecting. And the peon did a great job. He jumped over professor S.S. Roy and he was struggling and saying, "What are you doing? You idiot!" And he put him down on the sofa, pressed him down, and he said, "You need to be in bed. You are so sick. Do you want to commit suicide?"

Professor S.S. Roy's statement on the peon's note was, "Yes, it was wrong for me to come out. You just phone the postmaster to bring his car to take me back home, and inform the medical officer to come and check me. There seems to be something very wrong. Everybody is able to recognize it."

And then I entered the office where he was resting on the sofa, almost ready to die. I said, "Wait!" And I told the peon on the way, "Don't call anybody, for the car or for the doctor. There is no need. I will take care."

I said, "There is no need to die right now. One day you will have to die, but just take a few minutes' time. You just look at these notes...what you said to your wife."

He said, "You are a strange student, you would have killed me. Just another two persons more... And if they had said, 'You have died,' I would have believed it."

I said, "This is just in answer to our controversy."

If people go on saying something to you again and again you start believing it in spite of yourself. You may doubt the first time, but when it goes on being said continuously a belief arises in you, and you forget the doubt.

You have been told that you are sinners. You have been told that you are born in sin, and strange arguments have been provided to you why you are born in sin: because Adam and Eve disobeyed God. Now the Christian theologians say that although six thousand years have passed since Adam and Eve were removed by God from their place in the Garden of Eden, because they had disobeyed... He had

told them not to eat from two trees: one tree was the Tree of Knowledge, and the other was the Tree of Eternal Life.

I think Adam and Eve did exactly what anybody with any intelligence would do. These are the two things: wisdom and eternal life—what else do you want? And God is providing you with everything else, that means just chew like the buffalos, sit under trees. And the tree he had prohibited was an apple tree.

In the very fact of God's prohibiting, God dies as love, God dies as compassion. Otherwise, if God were the Father, he would have told the children, "These are the two trees that you should not forget: wisdom and eternal life." But this was reminded to Eve by the devil. The devil seems to be the first revolutionary in the world. He persuaded Eve.

I looked at this story from many angles. Why did he not persuade Adam? Because even if Adam is persuaded he will be obstructed. If Eve insists on not eating it, poor Adam is after all only the poor husband. Rather than persuading the husband he persuaded the wife. And since that time every advertisement is for the wife. Every church functions because of the support of the woman.

But his argument was right, and he had chosen the right person to persuade. He said, "God has prohibited you. Do you know the reason why? If you eat these two fruits, wisdom will make you enlightened, and eternal life.... And you will be just as powerful and as potent as God himself. And God is jealous of that; he does not want you to become gods. He wants you to remain worshippers—saints, sinners, but never gods. But these two fruits can make you real gods."

Strangely enough the religions which do not believe in God, their ultimate goal is freedom. And the religions that believe in God, their ultimate goal is salvation. A savior will come, you yourself are absolutely helpless. A messiah will come who will save you. They have been waiting for six thousand years, and he does not come. And once in a while if somebody gets insane enough and proclaims, "I am the one you are waiting for," they kill him.

It is a strange humanity. You are waiting for the person and if somebody tries.... It was not only Jesus. Jesus has become more prominent because a great religion arose behind him. There were other people:

THE SKY IS NOT SCRATCHED BY THE CLOUD

John the Baptist was killed because he proclaimed not even, "I am the prophet," but simply, "I am creating the right atmosphere for the prophet to come." He was beheaded. He proclaimed Jesus as the prophet for whom he had been making the way. And Jesus was crucified. The same has been the behavior all around the world.

Religions don't want you to be intelligent. The fruit of intelligence has been abandoned. If you become wise it is going against God. That's why all religions which believe in order and obedience don't preach meditation. These are very intricate matters. Why does Christianity not preach meditation? Why is there no place in Mohammedanism for meditation? For the simple reason that meditation is really both those trees together. It will bring you enlightenment and it will bring you an absolute, indubitable certainty that you are God, that everything is divine. In your godliness even the smallest grass leaf becomes divine, just as the biggest star. The whole universe becomes just a vibration of divine dance. But you have to feel it first in your heart, and all your so-called religions are driving you away from it: Pray to God!

I have heard about Michelangelo.... He was painting the ceiling of a famous cathedral. It was getting a little dark, and an old woman was praying to God, not knowing at all that above her on the ceiling Michelangelo was doing some painting. And he was getting tired lying on the long ladder. He listened to what this old woman was saying. She was asking God, "A little money won't be bad. I need it, because I don't have anybody to support me. You have taken everybody away." She was praying particularly to Mary, Jesus Christ's mother, because being a woman she will understand the troubles of an old woman.

Michelangelo, tired of his work, just wanted to enjoy the moment. He said, "I am listening to you. I am Jesus Christ."

The woman must have been a great woman. She said, "Shut up! I am talking to your mother directly!"

Michelangelo has written, "I could not believe it. I had offered, but she simply refused. She said, 'Shut up!' In the darkness she could not even see."

All these religions are trying to humiliate humanity. Their whole business and exploitation and oppression depend on you, your fear,

your greed, your death, your disease. If you start feeling yourself divine and can enjoy not only life but death too, with the same dance, what will be the purpose of the priests? And there are millions of them all over the world, just living like parasites. They may be Hindu, they may be Mohammedan, they may be Christian, they may belong to any religion, but priesthood is the ancientmost profession of parasites.

If you enter into yourself and find the truth, you will be surprised to see that what was within you was ignored with every effort, so that the exploitation could continue.

Buddha's attitude is that you are a buddha, it is not a question of achieving buddhahood. You are a buddha, all that you need is a mirror to see your face, your original face—a recognition, a remembrance. You have forgotten who you are.

This ignorance is being exploited by the churches, by the temples, by the priests, by the rabbis, by the pundits, by all kinds of theologians. They are creating barriers which are arbitrary, which if you want you can throw off in a single moment. But they have made you so much afraid—not believing in God means you will fall into hell.

I have come upon stories that in the Middle Ages priests used to be so emphatic about the tortures of hell, that you will be burned in an eternal fire; and yet you will not die—that solace they cannot give. You will be pulled out and put in the oven again, this side burned and that side burned…there are cases on record that many women used to faint just listening to these preachers. The whole idea was so ferocious, that you will never die and always in and out of the oven, a little rest and then back…

I have heard a story that Morarji Desai died. In a way it would be good. Since the Supreme Court has made him homeless, that would be one way to find a home. And thinking himself a great mahatma, he was convinced that he would reach to heaven, but what he saw was that he was being dragged into hell. He shouted, he tried hard to convince them, "I am the ex-prime minister of India, a great follower of Mahatma Gandhi. The whole day I have been spinning on the wheel. What do you mean? Hell is for sinners, not for mahatmas."

But the devils wouldn't listen. They said, "Be silent. You will be

given a choice because you have been a prime minister. This much favor we can do. There are three layers of hell, you can choose the one you want."

Seeing no possibility of escaping, Morarji agreed. They took him to the first section, and what he saw he could not believe: people were being beaten, blood was flowing. Death is impossible in hell, remember. That point you have always to remember: death is impossible, only torture. You cannot commit suicide. In hell that is not possible. You cannot escape, there is no exit.

Seeing that bloody place, people being tortured, beaten, he said, "I would rather like to see the other two before I choose."

In the second place, the Christian oven... People are being pulled in and out and cooked, and they are still alive! He said, "This is not possible for me. I am a vegetarian. I cannot even look at such a scene."

He was taken to the third. It looked a little better, not very much, but compared to the other two.... People were standing up to their neck in all kinds of shit, and drinking coffee and tea and Coca-Cola.

Everybody had to choose, whichever he wanted. He said, "This is not good, but what else to do? Those other two..." And he was a confirmed urine drinker for sixty years, so it was not very bad. It was good that he was accustomed and had rehearsed well. He had done his homework. He said, "I will choose this."

But he was not aware that it was only a coffee break. Just as he finished his coffee a bell rang and a devil shouted, "Now everybody stand on your head!"

All kinds of fear...if you don't believe in God. People think it is better to believe rather than to get into trouble. Sardar is thinking to himself about which of the three he would choose. Unfortunately there is no fourth, you have to choose between the three. And they were all nasty.

Man has been told by all religions that he is not what he should be. So try hard to be virtuous, try hard to be austere, try hard and pray continuously—a Mohammedan prays five times a day. And do all kinds of distortions of the body in the name of yoga, which is already a section of hell. The difference is just that here you are doing it on your own, in hell the devils do it for you—distort you, somebody is

pulling your leg, somebody is giving you a neck stretch...

And I know perfectly well what it means because my neck has been stretched. You have to say that it is absolutely okay, just to get them to stop. Otherwise if they go on stretching, soon your head will be off the body! You are suffering and you have to say that you are cured. They have put my body in traction. Traction was used for the first time by Christian missionaries and Christian churches in the Middle Ages for poor women who were declared to be witches. And finally that strategy of traction.... By chance it happened that somebody was suffering from a bad back when her body was stretched. For thirty years she had suffered from a bad back, suddenly her back settled down and there was no pain, and she could not believe it. From the church the traction machine has moved to the hospitals.

Here one of my very loving doctors, Dr. Hardikar—his name in English means Dr. Hard—worked on me. He is nice, but the things that he does.... The whole body is pulled, legs are pulled to one side, the head is pulled to the other side. Soon you start feeling that you are going to break up somewhere in between. That's why I say it is absolutely certain that in hell they have very primitive traction mechanisms—you don't die there. And my feeling is that the people who say they are cured are not really cured. It is my own experience. You have to say it, otherwise they are ready to give you more traction. Either you die or you say that you are cured—you don't have any other alternative.

Religion has been living on fear. And it has been creating disciplines like fasting—torture yourself in every possible way. The more you torture, the more God is happy with you. It is a strange argument, why does my being tortured make God happy? Is he a sadist? Is he mad, or what? My fasting makes him happy. I am suffering, I am hungry, my whole body is asking for food, and God is feeling very happy. I don't see any relationship between this and the idea that God is love—what kind of love?—that God is compassion. What kind of compassion? To achieve to him you have to go through all kinds of torture unnecessarily.

And once you have been convinced that God is a difficult goal to achieve...millions have tortured themselves that way, and not a

single one of them has ever reached to any realization of bliss. Those who have reached are a different kind of people. They don't say God is a goal—God is your nature! Just be natural; and silently, without even making the noise of footsteps, the buddha within you awakens.

Dōgen says, quoting Buddha,

If you want to understand the true meaning of the Buddha-nature,
you should correctly understand its momentary manifestations.

You are all its momentary manifestation. Everything in the world is its momentary manifestation. Somewhere nature has blossomed into a rose, somewhere it has become a bird flying in the sky, somewhere it is a pine tree reaching to the stars, and somewhere it is a human being. These are all momentary manifestations of the same nature.

The word 'buddha' comes from the Sanskrit root *buddh*. 'Buddh' means awareness. In any form you can become aware. But the human form is the easiest one from which to become aware. If you miss this opportunity you are missing something that you may find only after millions of years of search. Being a pine tree or a mountain rock—these are all manifestations. But no mountain has become a buddha, and no pine tree in its tremendous beauty has ever become enlightened. No animal, no bird, no tree, no sun, no moon, in all their beauty...they are manifestations of the same nature, but only man is capable of becoming aware of this self-nature. This double awareness—awareness of awareness—is man's grandeur. It is his treasure.

In the whole existence only man is capable, and if you miss this you don't know what you have missed. You have missed the greatest blissfulness that is possible, the greatest peace and silence and understanding, the greatest fearlessness and freedom.

Buddha's statement is that everything correctly understood is only a momentary manifestation of the same nature. A buddha is a recognition of this innermost life that throbs in everything—in the grass, in the water, in the clouds, in human beings. Wherever there is life, it is God in some form. This is a great declaration.

Buddha says,
When the right time comes, the Buddha-nature will manifest itself.
It has been a long tradition and controversy amongst the followers of

Buddha—"What does he mean by the right time?" It can be misunderstood, as Dōgen says. It can be misunderstood, that if it is going to happen at the right time then just enjoy your rented bicycle, why waste your time unnecessarily? Find a girlfriend or a boyfriend or any kind of friend, or just go to the movie. Do anything stupid, because at the right time buddhahood will appear—it does not matter, meanwhile, what you are doing.

People have used this statement to do anything they want—gambling, accumulating possessions, being rich, being powerful—because there is no need for them to make any special effort. At the right time the buddha-nature will manifest itself. This is one kind of misunderstanding.

By 'right time' Buddha does not mean that you have to postpone this moment, that when the right time comes.... It never comes. It is always the same time. And it is not something from outside that happens to you, it is something that blossoms within you.

So what is the meaning of 'the right time'? One misunderstanding is that you just go on doing the mundane activities. The other misunderstanding is to bring the right time close by austerities, by fasting, by prayer, by going to the church or to the temple, by standing on your head, by doing all kinds of contortions, by torturing yourself unnecessarily—to bring the right time close. That is another distortion, another misconception of Buddha's statement.

What is the right time? Dōgen says,

Many monks, both past and present, have believed that the phrase, "when the right time comes," means to wait for the Buddha-nature to manifest itself in the future. They think that if they continue training in the Way, the Buddha-nature will naturally manifest itself at the right time. Until that time comes, they mistakenly conclude that the Buddha-nature will not manifest itself, even should they visit a master in search of the Dharma or train diligently.

There is no need, according to this misconception, to go to a master. But the whole misunderstanding is about the right time, what is the right time. Every moment is the right time. Just you need a little courage to risk your knowledgeability, to risk your ego, to put at stake everything that you think is valuable. Search within yourself for the

THE SKY IS NOT SCRATCHED BY THE CLOUD

only thing that you can neither borrow from anybody, nor give to anybody. That is your nature. And that nature is always in the present. Hence the present is the right time. Neither yesterday nor tomorrow—today! This very moment you can become a buddha.

Based on this false conclusion, they meaninglessly return to the ordinary world and vainly wait for the right time to come.

The right time is not to come. It has always been here. Dōgen says,

The words, "When the right time comes," means that the right time has already *come.*

In fact it never comes, never goes. It is always here. The ocean remains, the fish is born and one day disappears. Just like a wave—a little more solid, but just like a wave. The sky remains; once in a while it is clouded, but those clouds come and go, leaving the sky unscratched.

Talking about our buddha-nature is talking about our inner, interiormost being, our very sky. Our thoughts are just clouds, they come and go. Our emotions are just smoke...momentary. Everything is momentary. Our childhood goes, our youth goes, our old age goes, our life itself goes. In all this only one thing remains the same, and that is the present awareness. On this account Dōgen is saying that the right time has already been here. You don't have to wait for it.

There can be no doubt about this. Even should doubts arise, they are nothing but the manifestation of the Buddha-nature in ourselves.

These are the beautiful contributions to the world of those who are seekers of the mysteries. Even doubts are our nature, so they are nothing to be condemned. If a doubt arises it is a cloud that has come into the sky, but the sky is not going to be scratched by the cloud. The cloud will disappear; as it has arisen it will be gone.

And anyway, whatever happens in the world is part of the universe. It is immensely significant to understand that even doubts are our buddha-nature.

If the right time were something which came, *the Buddha-nature would not come.*

Because if it is a question of coming and going, like seasons...the rain comes and goes, the winter comes and goes, the spring comes and goes. If buddha-nature is dependent on time, then as it will come

it will go. It cannot be dependent on any causality, it cannot be dependent on any time. The fact is it is already there, only you have to be awake enough to recognize it. The right time is this time, this moment! Zen's insistence on this moment is immense. It does not allow any postponement.
This is because the right time has already come; the Buddha-nature has already manifested itself. This fact is quite clear, for there has never been a right time that has not come, nor a Buddha-nature which has not manifested itself.
It is really saying.... An ancient Zen story: A man was known as a master thief, because he had never been caught in his life, and he had stolen from every palace, from every rich house. In fact the situation had come to such a point that people bragged about it—that the master thief has entered in their house.

This master thief met Rinzai, who looked into his eyes and said, "Don't be worried. Whatever you are doing, do it totally, and you are expressing buddha-nature."

But the man said, "You don't know what I am doing."

He said, "Don't bother. Whatever you are doing...I know you—you are a master thief. I am really jealous of you. I am not such a great master as far as meditation is concerned. You are a greater master as far as stealing is concerned. Just do it totally, and you will find your buddhahood in your totality."

There have been butchers who have become masters, and their masters did not prevent them from the profession of butchery because they were so perfect, they were so total in whatever they were doing. This is the only religion in the whole world which allows you everything. Do it totally, with absolute awareness, and all your activities become buddha-activities. There is no need to change what you are doing. If you are painting, then be a painter so deeply that you disappear and only the painting remains. If you are a musician, drown yourself in your music, so that the music remains but you are not. And your buddhahood will manifest in thousands of ways.

This is the only religious approach in the whole world and the whole of man's history that accepts all man's activities without rejecting anything. You can make everything a prayer, everything a

THE SKY IS NOT SCRATCHED BY THE CLOUD

meditation, everything your offering to the universe.

A Zen poet:

> *The raging wind's companion:*
> *In the sky,*
> *the single moon.*

These are pictorial haikus. Sitting silently, a meditator opens his eyes and sees the raging wind's companion in the sky: the single moon. But the moon does not move, does not waver because of the raging wind. If you can find yourself the center of the cyclone you have found the moon—no raging wind, no thought, no emotion, nothing can disturb it. It is undisturbable.

A haiku by Issa:

> *Lost in bamboo,*
> *but when moon lights—*
> *my house.*

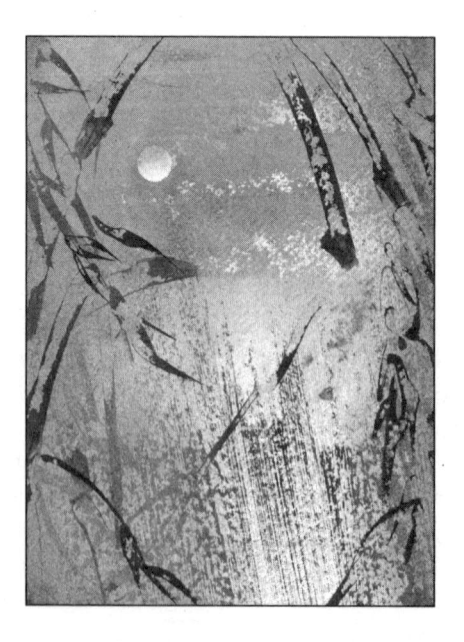

Just fragments of experience. Nobody will call them great poetry; they are not of the same category. They have their own category. What he is saying is,

"In silent meditation, I saw...*lost in bamboo, but when moon lights —my house.*"

Just a picture...and one becomes a mirror. This haiku is just a mirror of a house, hidden in the thick grove of bamboos; and the moon comes, and suddenly the house that was hidden in the darkness becomes light.

A haiku by Bashō:

*A cloud,
trying to enwrap the moonbeams,
A monsoon shower.*

Enjoying everything—the moon, the cloud, the monsoon shower—because everything to the meditator becomes so divine that it is an expression and manifestation of the same original source.

Maneesha has asked:

*Our Beloved Master,
It does not seem so difficult to drop the notions of right and wrong as far as some society's morality is concerned. More tricky is to drop the feeling that enlightenment is "right," and that until I realize it, I am somehow "wrong."
Beloved Master, could You put me right?*

Maneesha, you are right. Nobody can put you wrong! As you are, you are the buddha. It does not matter that you are sitting in a different posture. It does not matter that you are a woman and not a man. It does not matter that you don't walk like Buddha, you don't talk like Buddha. Whatever you do, you cannot do anything that is not a manifestation of buddhahood.

To understand this point is to reach a great height of consciousness. The thief is fulfilling his part, he just has to do it perfectly. And if you are not a buddha—that is just an idea, a cloud that has

covered the moon; it will pass away. Clouds don't remain forever.

And I can understand, Maneesha. It will remain difficult until you become enlightened. But every night you become enlightened, and again you forget. What to do with your impossibility, your stubbornness, your insistence that "No, I am not a buddha"? It is up to you. If you insist, that too is a manifestation of buddhahood. That is what Zen is all about—to tell you that whatever you do, just do with full awareness. You *are* a buddha, you cannot be otherwise. It is impossible not to be a buddha. You can doubt it, you can deny it, but the doubt and the denial are all potentialities of your buddhahood.

No tree denies, no bird denies, no animal doubts. It is only man who has doubts, who cannot accept, "Such a poor creature like me, and a buddha?" He is perfectly ready to worship a buddha. He is perfectly ready to pray before man-made stone statues. But this seems to be too much, to accept the fact that, "I am a buddha."

And I say unto you that it is simply a question of getting tired of not being a buddha—that's how it happened to me. I tried and tried and tried, and then finally I said, "It is better to be a buddha without effort." And since then I have been a buddha. Not for a single moment have I been otherwise. Not for a single moment has any doubt arisen.

It just takes a little courage. Traditionally you have been discouraged, you have been humiliated. All that is needed is to revolt against all humiliation, to revolt against all false ideas imposed upon you, to express your dignity with joy. And to be a buddha is not a comparison, so there is no question of ego. It is not that if Maneesha becomes a buddha, then Chitten will become an ordinary human being sitting by the side of Maneesha, a buddha. Chitten is a buddha from the very beginning. He is a senior buddha! If you become a buddha today, there will be many who have become a buddha days ago. Yesterday a few became, the day before yesterday a few became. There is still time to give recognition to yourself, and express your dignity, and reject all ideas of humiliation and all ideas of destroying your dignity.

My whole effort here is not to train you for being buddhas, but just to give you courage so that you can accept your buddhahood without any fear.

And as the fear disappears, the clouds disappear, and the full moon in the night....

Maneesha, I will try again today. Let us see whether I can put you right or not. I have been trying for thirty years continuously. I put people right and the moment I am gone they fall apart. In my presence they recognize that they are buddhas. In my absence a doubt arises. Maneesha sitting in her room, "My God, I, a poor girl, and a buddha? I have not renounced a kingdom, I have not done great austerities, I have not tortured myself, I have not disciplined myself."

Just today Shunyo told me that Zareen wanted her to wear a sari. Now the sari fits perfectly well with the Indian woman's curvature. It is very rare for a Western woman to look graceful in a sari—she looks a little weird. I cannot help it, it does not mean that I am denying, just the buddha has gone a little weird. And I had told Shunyo long ago, because once before she had tried a sari, and I had told her, "This is not for you. You are too long for it, and too straight!" On Zareen it fits. In fact, Zareen cannot use a robe. In the commune she had come to see me in a robe, and she looked like a balloon! I could not believe it—what has happened to her?

No Indian woman will look right in a robe, particularly a Zareen-type woman. The sari is a very inventive art on the part of Zareen-type women. It hides all unnecessary growth and keeps them tied together, otherwise they may fall and spread all over the place! And out of love she insisted—she told Shunyo, "It will take only five minutes." And Shunyo was telling me, "It took one hour to put the sari on me." And Zareen afterwards said to me, "She is exaggerating, it takes only five minutes!"

You are a buddha. It takes only five minutes! But you go on insisting every day, again and again asking, "Do you think I am also a buddha?" Or, "Do you think I am still a buddha?" You were a buddha yesterday, you are a buddha today, you will be a buddha tomorrow. Whatever you do, it does not matter. Your buddhahood is your very life.

You can change your clothes, you can change your accents, you can change your behavior, it does not matter. So many manifestations of buddhahood—it is a beautiful variety. If all looked like Buddha,

just sitting under every tree, think of the boredom. Wherever you go you meet the same Buddha; wherever you look, under every tree, Buddha is sitting! You would commit suicide—that it is better to die than to live in a city where everybody is behaving like Buddha.

But still I insist that you are a buddha. I am not saying to you that you have to behave like Buddha; you have to be spontaneously yourself. And honestly and totally being yourself is what buddha-nature means.

Before we again enter into our buddha-nature, a little laughter will be alright. Before risking, it is always good to laugh, because you may die when I say die. If you are really total, you will die. Then Nivedano can go on hitting his drum…you will not come back. But you come back so quickly that I suspect you don't die. You try hard, that I know, and everybody is managing to get in the right comfortable position. That is not allowed. When you are dying, die! That does not mean, "Now what comfortable position…" Others will take care when you are finished. But you know perfectly well that it is only a rehearsal, the real drama has not started yet, and there is no hurry. Anyway you can die tomorrow.

Zabriski takes Gorgeous Gloria out on a date. They are sitting in a quiet corner of the bar, sipping martinis, when Zabriski leans over and whispers in Gloria's ear, "What would you say if I asked you to marry me?"

"Nothing," replies Gloria. "I can't talk and laugh at the same time!"

It is monsoon in Poona, and Swami Deva Coconut meets Swami Veet Herschel on M.G. Road.

"Hi, Coconut!" says Herschel. "I have been meaning to ask you, can I have back the umbrella that you borrowed from me?"

"Oh, sorry," says Coconut. "I lent it to a friend of mine. Did you want it?"

"Not for myself," replies Herschel. "But the swami I borrowed it from says the owner wants it back!"

A Polack is badly injured in a car crash and he has to have a brain transplant. A team of surgeons put him to sleep, remove his brain, and go into the next room to get a new one. But when they return to the operating room, the Polack is gone.

The police search everywhere for him but without success—he has vanished. The doctors contact the international police and they check throughout the world for a brainless Pole.

Finally, five years later, they find him. He is wearing silly robes and a big hat and is living in the Vatican!

General Brahmachapatti has been in Ruby Hall Clinic for a couple of weeks for a minor operation. The nurses are fed up with him. He is always complaining about the food and the service, waking up the nurses in the middle of the night, demanding cups of hot chocolate, and so on.

One morning a nurse comes into his room and says, "Good morning, general. Please take down your pyjamas and turn over—I need to take your temperature."

"But nurse," protests the general, "I always have the thermometer in my mouth, not my ass. Why this change?"

"This morning," explains the nurse, "we need a really accurate temperature, so that the lab can make an analysis."

The general grumpily agrees, takes down his pyjamas, turns over, and raises his bum in the air.

"Now, general," says the nurse, making the insertion, "this is a special thermometer and it needs to be left quite a long time to get an accurate result. So don't move until I come back."

In the next few hours many people come into the general's room, but all of them just gasp and leave quickly in embarrassment. Finally, the general's wife comes to visit him.

She walks in and stares at him in amazement, not knowing what to say.

"What is the matter with you, woman?" thunders the general. "Haven't you ever seen someone having their temperature taken before?"

"Yes, darling, I have," stammers his wife, "but not with a banana!"

THE SKY IS NOT SCRATCHED BY THE CLOUD

Now, Nivedano…

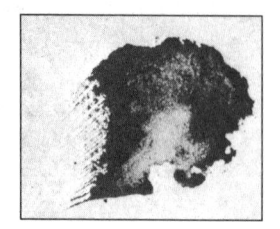

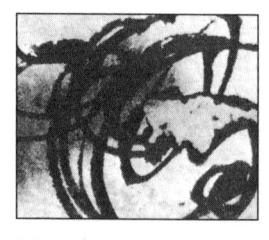

Nivedano…

Be silent…
Close your eyes…
Feel the body frozen, no movement.
Collect your consciousness inward,
close to the very center.
The deeper you go,
the more you will find the realization,
the recognition of a buddha.
In this silent moment
there are only ten thousand buddhas
sitting here.
Make this experience as deep as possible.

DŌGEN

And keep it alive in your ordinary activities
twenty-four hours. Every action
should be a reminder that you are a buddha...
and your action is a manifestation of your nature.
Don't act unnaturally,
don't act artificially, don't be a hypocrite.
Just be natural and you are a buddha.
So gather your consciousness
more deeply,
to crystallize it.

Nivedano...

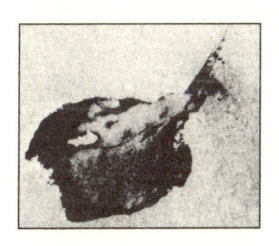

Rest...
relax...
really die.
Don't be worried what happens afterwards.
The world will continue...you don't be worried,
just die.
As the body is lying dead,
you can enter into yourself more easily.
Unidentified with the body
you can see the open sky inside.
This is your eternity.
This is your reality.
This is it.
All else is commentary.
This experience is the only truth.
Such a beautiful silence...
Such a blissful evening...

THE SKY IS NOT SCRATCHED BY THE CLOUD

You are the most fortunate beings
on the earth this moment.
Realize the dignity of it
and the honor of it.
Here my work is not for you to search
for the buddha,
so stop searching...
and just look within.
He is sitting there inside you.

Nivedano...

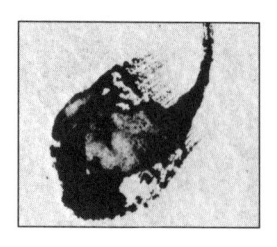

Come back,
but not in a hurry.
Somebody may have died.
Just don't disturb the dead.
Those who are still alive,
come back. And sit silently for a few minutes
to remind yourself of the experience
you have passed through.

You are a rare assembly.
It used to be in the past...
those days were golden,
when there were hundreds of assemblies
like this...
recognizing their nature
and remembering it
in their actions and manifestations.

That golden world has disappeared.
But at least for you
this moment opens up the whole glory of being.

Okay, Maneesha?
Yes, Beloved Master.

I have put you right?
Yes, Beloved Master.

Now can we celebrate this great gathering of buddhas?
Yes, Beloved Master.

LIVE ONE DAY AS A BUDDHA

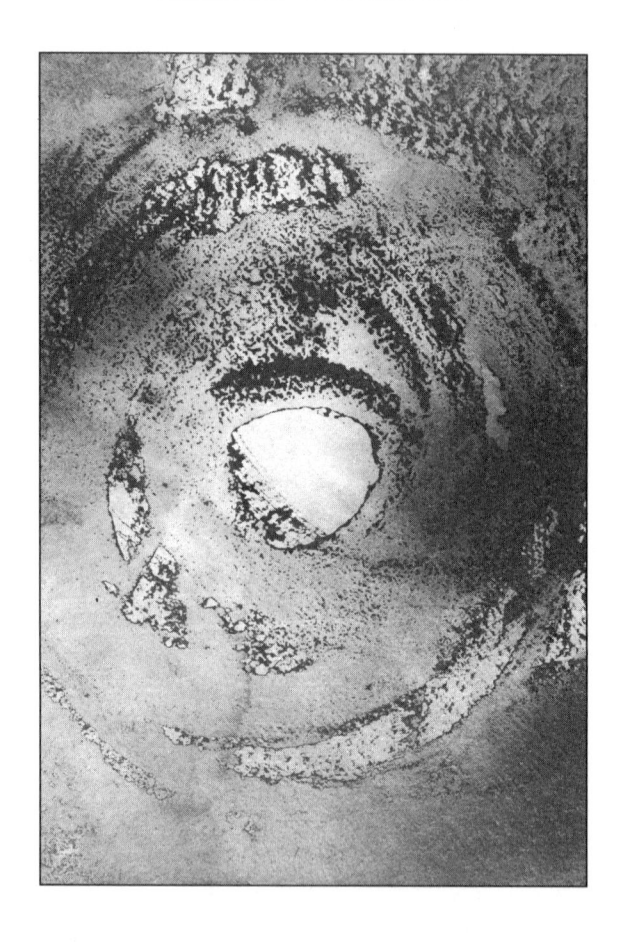

The moon in the water;
Broken and broken again,
still it is there.

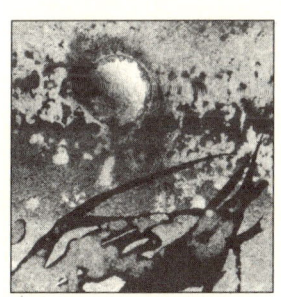

*Our Beloved Master,
Dōgen wrote:*
Practice is identical with expression, and vice versa. To express the Way all day is to practice the Way all day. In other words, we practice something impracticable and express something inexpressible....

Each day's life should be esteemed; the body should be respected. So if we can really get the Buddhist function even in a day, such a single day can be said to be more valuable than countless idle lives.

Therefore, before we have realized the Way, we must not idle away even a single day. Such a single day is too precious a treasure to be compared with a fine jewel. Ancient wise persons held it dearer than their body and life.

We must think quietly that a fine jewel and a rare gem, though lost, may be acquired again, but that a single day in a hundred years of life, once lost, never returns. No matter how skillful we may be, it is impossible to bring back even a single day of the past. No history book says that it is possible....

Why does time deprive us of our training, daily and lifelong? Why has time a grudge against us? It is, unfortunately, because we have ever neglected our practice....

Without looking forward to tomorrow every moment, you must think only of this day and this hour. Because tomorrow is difficult and unfixed, and difficult to know, you must think of following the Way while you live today.... You must concentrate on Zen practice without wasting time, thinking that there is only this day and this hour. After that, it becomes truly easy. You must forget about the good and the bad of your nature, the strength or weakness of your power.

Maneesha, before I start talking about Dōgen I have to make a few statements. One is about Zen master Niskriya. He had fallen so low in the West that yesterday I called him Skinhead, rather than Stonehead. And he had come perfectly dressed, like a Zen master. Today he is not wearing his robe. It does not matter even if you become a skinhead, back here you are again Sekitō—the Zen Master Stonehead. So cut your hair and put on your Zen master's dress, with your staff—it may be needed any time. I have been missing you for so long, there was nobody here to hit people. And you should not do such a thing—growing hair on a stonehead. Be ashamed of yourself.

In Germany nobody may have noticed it, but here everybody will notice, "What happened to Zen Master Sekitō?" He got lost. Everybody gets lost, particularly back in Germany where real idiots, very authentic idiots, live. He fell from the heights of being a Zen master into a skinhead.

Just shave your head and be your own self with your Zen stick and Zen master's robe. You are still a buddha. It does not matter that you traveled to Germany, your buddha-nature is intact. That has been our whole discussion on Dōgen's sutras. You can even go to Germany, even become a member of the German parliament—you cannot fall more than that—still you will be a buddha.

And second, to Zareen. She has been moving around the ashram the whole day in her robe to prove the fact that, yes, she does look

like a balloon. I was hoping that she would have courage enough to come here like that, but she has come again here with a sari.

A balloon is beautiful. Just all you need is to make a few windows here and there to see who is inside. She is a great woman, and that's why she was not afraid. The whole day everybody was talking about the balloon. I was sitting in my room, listening to all kinds of gossip about her coming in a balloon. And here I see she is sitting in her usual dress, looking so beautiful.

The sari has a magic. The people who discovered the sari must have been very aesthetic. They wanted their women to look like Khajuraho statues—round, full.

The idea arose in the West, with women's liberation, that the woman has to look like a man; she has to wear pants. It proves a strange psychological fact. Because of her dress, she started losing the curves that she always had in the past, even in the West. She started becoming a straight line, flat. Looking at a Western woman with pants and a shirt, with a cigarette in her hand, you have to think for a moment whether she is a woman or a man. That kind of confusion never arises in the East. A woman is a woman, a man is a man. And the woman has not to imitate man; otherwise she will destroy herself. She has to be herself. She is not inferior, she is simply different.

The liberation movement emphasizes the wrong point. There is no question of equality. You don't ask for equality between two different things. A woman has her own uniqueness, she has not to imitate man. And by imitation, remember, you will not even be a woman, you will be only a second-rate man.

The sari gives a certain freedom to the Indian woman to grow curves. She is more explorable. In the Western woman, what are you going to explore? She is just as she looks with clothes. But the Indian woman is totally different. You are going to be surprised... She has something interesting hidden behind the sari. It is a great invention.

But don't imitate because then you look very weird. Just think of Zareen in pants and a shirt; she would become the most weird animal around. Right now she is so beautiful.

But there is always a desire to be in other people's dresses, in other people's lifestyles. And one does not know that this is the way that

one becomes lost and forgets the way home. Never, for a single moment, be imitative. Just be yourself. And not only be yourself; Dōgen says, "Respect yourself. Respect your body."

These are the beautiful things that Zen has brought into the history of mankind, particularly in the history of consciousness.

Dōgen wrote:
Practice is identical with expression, and vice versa.
He is talking about an authentic man; what in Zen language is called the original man. His practice is identical with his expression. There are not two persons in him, there is only a single individuality. Silent, it is the same. In expression, in manifestation—in any possible way—it is the still the same. Raising my hand, I am as much a buddha as without raising it.

Practice is identical with expression, and vice versa. But this is not true about the man that has come to exist in this contemporary world. He says something, he thinks something, he desires something; he really wants something else. He is simply a confusion. The modern man is a confused buddha. He does not know that to be one he has to drop many masks. All those masks are to deceive people, to create a certain respectability, a reputation.

But deep down you are dishonest. There is nothing wrong in being dishonest, but then express it, and be clear: "But I am not an honest man, don't rely on me." And you will feel a certain freedom that you have never known. When your expression and your being are one, you have the whole sky as your freedom. Otherwise, one is tied down to his lies.

It is said about George Gurdjieff… To explain to his disciples, he developed a certain technique. He could laugh with half of his face, and at the same time he could be sad with the other half. It is very difficult, I don't know how he managed it. But he had lived with very ancient tribes in Turkestan, in the Soviet Union's very backward parts where people are still as primitive as you can conceive. His father died early so he had to live with first one tribe, then another tribe. He was only nine years old but he started learning—because

those tribes steal, play music, do magic, heal people. They are moving people; they don't have houses, stability. They enjoy traveling, they are vagabonds.

But he turned this into a great opportunity to learn all their tricks. One of their tricks was that they could manage to divide their face in two. And while teaching his students, once in a while he would do that trick. Somebody is sitting by his right side and somebody on his left side; and on one side he will look very angry, and on the other side very loving and peaceful. And they both report to each other what is going on. One says that he is very loving and very peaceful. The other says, "Peaceful? He looks very dangerous, violent, murderous. He looked at me with an eye that I am not going to forget for months."

When it was reported to him, Gurdjieff would say, "This is what I want you to understand: modern man has many faces."

You should watch. When you meet your wife and you say, "Darling," do you really mean it? "My sweetheart"—do you really mean it? When you are saying those words, are you remembering some other woman? Unfortunately, you have to say these words to the woman whom you want to kill. But you are not that courageous either. When you see your servant, have you the same face as when you see your boss? Just watch the changes in your face. You are not a single unity, integrated.

Whether clouds come and go, whether clouds are white or black, does not matter. The moon remains shining the same. The clouds come and go, they don't leave any scratches on the moon. But every cloud—that means every mask that you wear—leaves its marks on you.

So I have seen people laughing, but I see that they are almost at the point of weeping. They are hiding their tears behind a fake smile. And people are doing the opposite also.

I used to live with one of my relatives. A faraway relative of my relative had come for treatment of his wife. The wife died, and naturally my relatives had to show all kinds of mourning. They were

really not at all concerned with it. In fact they were happy that she was gone because, with her, the whole family was suffering unnecessarily. The moment she died her husband went back to his city, but people used to come to the house. It was just a conformity, a social pattern, to show your sympathy. So the woman of the house was in a trouble, because when you don't have any tears...it is very difficult. And each day it might happen ten times.

I used to stay out in the garden. She told me, "Keep a bell here with you."

I said, "For what?"

She said, "Whenever somebody comes, you just ring the bell. Then I will pull down my *ghoonghat* and start crying. It will be false, but what else to do?"

The sari has that great quality also. You can pull down your ghoonghat...inside you may not be crying but you can pretend to be in immense sadness and misery.

I said, "This is a great strategy. But beware of me."

She said, "What do you mean?"

I said, "I can ring the bell at the wrong person."

She said, "No, you should not do that. I have been harassed, tortured, for months taking care of that woman, who was only a faraway relative." But in India, faraway relatives are still relatives. Sometimes one does not know in what way a person is a relative, but you have to take care of them if they proclaim they are. Some cousin of your cousins...

I said, "Don't be worried."

She used to remain inside the house. Whenever somebody came, I simply gave her the bell, and she would immediately pull down her ghoonghat. There is no word for ghoonghat in English—it is part of the sari. But you all understand what it is. It means pulling your tent down a little so that your face is hidden, so nobody can see what actually is happening on your face. And you can pretend anything.

So for a few days I managed it. One day her husband came and I rang the bell. That was so hilarious that even today I cannot forget it. She pulled her tent down and started weeping as if somebody had died. The husband said, "Has somebody died again?"

She looked through the ghoonghat, and seeing that it was her husband, she said, "No, it is... I knew that sometime he was going to deceive me, but I never thought that he would shock you. Where is he?"

They both came out and she said, "This is not good. My husband is not coming in the house to sympathize or to mourn."

I said, "He looked so sad that I thought that somebody must have died. And it is better to make you aware that your husband is looking very sad. This is not the moment to desire a loving word; this is a moment to weep and cry with him."

The husband said, "What do you mean, I was looking sad?"

I said, "Now, don't provoke me. By nature, your face is such that it seems somebody has died. I don't usually say it, because what is the point? You are not responsible. This is the face you have got."

He said, "Really, I look so sad?"

I said, "You can ask anybody. I can bring a few witnesses from the neighborhood. Everybody knows that you are very sad and very serious and worried."

He said, "No need to bring the neighbors"—because he knew I would convince a few people. "I will try to make my face better. I will try once in a while to laugh, smile."

I said to him, "It is not a question of trying. In the first place, you shave your moustache. You have a strange moustache that makes you look like a clown."

He said, "You live in my house and you always create trouble. Now, I love my moustache, I cannot shave it."

I said, "It is up to you. But this is what makes your face look so sad. Get some false moustache. Glue it on whenever you want a moustache, but this moustache won't do." He certainly had a moustache, drooping all over the face.

But everybody is having different kinds of faces, and it has become almost an autonomous process; they don't have to change. Just you see a man walking with his wife and you know with whom he is walking. You don't have to inquire, "Are you married?" And look at him with his girlfriend and again you don't have to inquire.

Just their faces, with so much freedom, joy—momentary, but even a momentary phenomenon makes them happy, changes their faces.

A seeker, according to Dōgen, has to remember his integrity. In every situation, his practice and his expression should be identical.

To express the Way all day is to practice the Way all day.
To express the Way all day.... I have told you you are all buddhas. Reluctantly, you accept it. Deep down, you know who you are. Somebody is a doctor, somebody is an attorney, somebody is a rickshaw walla. "A buddha pulling a rickshaw? My God, this has never happened."

But because I am saying it, and you love me, and you trust me, you say, "Okay." Right now, at least inside Buddha Hall anyway, you will not be allowed to bring your rickshaw or your rented bicycle. What is the harm in being a buddha? But once out of the hall you start having second thoughts, "Where am I going? I am a buddha? Then what am I doing smoking a cigarette?" Now just think—a buddha smoking a cigarette? Inconceivable.

If you want to know your essential self you have to express it all the way, all the day, in every smallest expression. It does not matter—even if you are pulling a rickshaw, you can pull the rickshaw with deep compassion, with love, with respect for the passenger, with care about other people in the traffic.

I am making buddhahood simple and at the same time very complicated. It is very easy to sit under a bodhi tree in the lotus posture and declare to the world, "I am a buddha." The real thing is when you are sitting by the side of your wife, constantly afraid, "One never knows when she will start nagging."

When I was telling you the story yesterday about "Nag, nag, nag," Miyah Farookh was pulling Zareen's sari, with each nag reminding her, "Just know what you have been doing all your life."

He is a very unique child. It is unfortunate that he is missing these two days otherwise he would have enjoyed. When, in a story, the sun said to Mikhail Gorbachev, "Now I'm in the West—fuck you!" he rolled down on the ground. He understood that this is great. And when I was telling a story about an advocate—that he is a lion in the court—even before I could say it, I heard him saying silently,

"In the home he is a rat." But every husband is in the same situation.

We need a world...a new man, a new woman, a new child, who has intelligence. Not to imitate, not to deceive, but to stand on his own with power and integrity. Even if it means that he will be condemned by the whole world, it does not matter. What ultimately matters is that you have your own face.

In other words, we practice something impracticable and express something inexpressible.

Remember it. When you are watering the rose bush, remember that its beauty, its flowers, its greenness is so profound, but it is inexpressible. Never forget that this experience of beauty is as inexpressible as the experience of your own self. If you just watch, you will find in your life, in each moment, things which are inexpressible. You have just become accustomed. Your becoming accustomed is just a forgetfulness.

Socrates remembered at the last moment of his life, "I don't know anything. Let it be remembered by the coming generations that I didn't know."

He was proclaimed by the Oracle of Delphi as the wisest man in the whole world. The people who had heard the oracle went to Socrates with great joy to tell him what the oracle had said. Socrates said, "Just please go and tell the oracle that this time the oracle has been wrong. As far as I know, I know nothing."

The people were sad. They went back to Delphi and told the oracle what Socrates had said. "He says, 'I don't know anything at all,' and you call him the wisest man in the world."

The oracle laughed and said, "Exactly because of this I call him the wisest man of the world—because he has come to the point where he knows that he knows nothing."

Only in this space your potentiality blossoms to its totality. It is not knowledge—it is so deep that you can call it a heartbeat, or, perhaps more deeply, you can call it the heartbeat of the universe itself. But you cannot call it knowledge. And there is no way to express it.

If you can remember this in your everyday affairs... Do you think you know your child? Have you ever thought about it; that your

child has come through you but he is a mystery coming from the beyond? You cannot possess him. You can take care of this mysterious expression of life, you can love him. But you should not condition him, you should not take him to the church or to the synagogue or to the temple to start the conditioning process which destroys his innocence and takes away his authenticity.

I have heard about a rabbi and a bishop. They lived next to each other and both were very competitive. They had to be, to convince their congregations: "Who is greater?" One day the rabbi looked over the fence, and could not believe what he saw. The bishop was pouring water on a Cadillac.

He said, "What are you doing?"

The bishop said, "I am giving the Christian ceremony to my new Cadillac—baptism. You don't know about these things."

The rabbi was very humiliated. The next day he found a Rolls Royce. It was a question, not only of himself but of his religion. When the bishop was in his garden he came out with some garden shears and started cutting the exhaust pipe. The bishop was shocked. He said, "What are you doing? A new Rolls Royce and you are destroying it."

The rabbi said, "You don't understand these things. This is called circumcision. From now on this Rolls Royce is Jewish."

That's what we are doing even to human beings. We don't allow a child to be himself. And that is causing all the misery in the world: that nobody is himself. Everybody is imitating somebody else, everybody has become a carbon copy of somebody else, everybody is almost like a broken record that has been used for centuries. Nobody has newness, freshness—one's own originality. Remember, when you see a child, that he is as inexpressible as you. When you see a pine tree, don't forget it.

This is what Dōgen means…practicing real religion; remembering in every action, thought, silence, always, that it is inexpressible, it is mysterious; that we are living in a miracle world. All our explanations are just consolations. Nothing is explained, either by science or by religion. For thousands of years religion has tried to befool people

by giving them explanations about the creation of the world, about God—how he created the world in six days, how he has taken away the paradise of man and woman. Unless you are very torturous towards yourself you will never be allowed back into the garden. And people believed it, people have lived according to it.

Different religions have been propagating different superstitions. Now slowly slowly science has come to take the place of religion. But do you know that every scientific explanation is momentary? What it says today it may not say tomorrow. Every research goes on deeper, and old explanations become out of date. Old medicines which were thought to be helping people are found to have been harming people. But as long as the superstitions continued everybody believed, even the doctors believed.

This is true about what they believe even today, because tomorrow it may not be the same. Now we are full of scientific superstitions. Science has not changed man's being. Just as religion has failed, science has failed to remind him that everything is an immense mystery. The very effort to find an explanation is wrong—just love it, live it, dance it. Don't waste your time in finding explanations. This is the Zen attitude.

Each day's life should be esteemed; Do you ever esteem your life? *...the body should be respected.* Do you respect your body? It serves you for seventy years without any salary, without going on a strike, without taking a *morcha*—a protest march—against you. But you have not even thought that some respect is due, that your body needs to be valued.

So if we can really get the Buddhist function even in a day, such a single day can be said to be more valuable than countless idle lives.
That's why I say, every night, these few moments are the most valuable moments in your life. And every evening, when so many living buddhas gather here, this place becomes the most important in the whole world—the spiritual capital of the world. Because nowhere are so many people meditating together. Nowhere are so many people digging so deep that they can find the very life source, the eternity, the deathlessness.

Dōgen is right. Even if we can live one day, just twenty-four

hours, as a buddha—reminding ourselves continuously that each of our actions should reflect a buddha—that single day becomes more precious than thousands of lives. And if you can do it for one day, who is preventing you from doing it every day? If you can be a buddha here, why can you not be a buddha anywhere else? It is simply a question of being alert, respectful of existence, loving; of being utterly contented with the flowers, with the birds, with the trees, with the stars. Such a tremendous universe is given to you and you never pay any attention to it. You never give any gratitude. The whole beauty of existence is available to you, and you are reading a third-rate yellow newspaper that you have been reading since the morning. And not having anything else to do, you start reading it again.

It happened that a man used to live next to my house who was retired, senile, and everybody thought him mad except me. He was very friendly towards me. His only love affair was the newspaper, and because many newspapers used to come to me, he would come every morning—sometimes when I was not even awake he would knock. And I would give him anything—ten-year-old magazines—and he would say, "Thank you."

I was amazed. I said to him, "You know perfectly well that this magazine is ten years old."

He said, "What does it matter? To me it is new, I have not read it before. People think me mad. Do you think I'm mad?"

I said, "Certainly not, your argument is absolutely right. For you it is not ten years old, it is fresh, because you have not read it."

But he reminded me that his whole concern was newspapers. In a day he would come two, three times to ask me, "Has anything new come? The evening newspaper?"

I asked him, "Is the newspaper the whole world?"

He said, "What else to do? I am retired from my work. People think I am mad, so I don't have any social life. People avoid me. You are the only person who will talk with me, who respects me, who accepts me as a human being. And what else is there? I am only waiting for death."

The day he said to me, "I am only waiting for death," I started to think about everyone—What are you doing? Somebody is running a business, somebody is accumulating money, somebody is becoming more powerful in politics.

But do you understand that you are moving towards death? Each moment death is coming closer and closer. And have you gathered anything that you will be able to take with you when you die? Except meditation, you cannot take any of your possessions with you. All that is outside of you will be left behind. Only the inner flame...if you have found it, if you have become conscious of it, then there is no death for you. But if you are not conscious of it you will think also, as others are thinking, that you are dead.

It is simply a question of thinking. If you know yourself exactly, you are never dead. But you never go inwards. You have simply forgotten that there is an immense space waiting for you, and that is your real home. All our efforts here in this Buddha Hall are efforts to make you acquainted again with your real home, which will not be burned on a funeral pyre, which will remain until eternity, in different forms or in formlessness. That is your buddhahood.

But to make it a constant remembrance you have to work out a certain discipline. The discipline is simple: remember always that everything is a miracle, everything is inexpressible. This whole world is so mysterious that you don't have to read detective novels and you don't have to go to see movies. If you can understand this silence, you will love to find spaces where you can be silent again and again. If you can touch the waters of life within you, you would love...in your whole day, whenever you can find just a moment, sipping the tea...you would love to look in, to see whether those waters of life are still flowing. One becomes accustomed, slowly slowly, to the eternity of oneself. But whether you know it or not, it is there.

Such a single day is too precious a treasure to be compared with a fine jewel. Ancient wise persons held it dearer than their body and life. We must think quietly that a fine jewel and a rare gem, though lost, may be acquired again, but that a single day in a hundred years of life, once lost, never returns.

Remember that not a single moment will come back again into your hands. That which is gone is gone forever.

Take out the whole juice of every moment. The moment will be gone; but the juice, the experience, the mystery, the fragrance of it will surround you. And every day it will become deeper and deeper, thicker and thicker. A day will come when you will not be afraid to declare that you are a buddha. It will come on its own, spontaneously; a sudden lightning and you will say, "My God—what have I been doing up to now? I *am* a buddha and this whole universe *is* my home. As much as I need it, it needs me too."

We are part of one tremendous mystery.

No matter how skillful we may be, it is impossible to bring back even a single day of the past. No history book says that it is possible.

Why does time deprive us of our training, daily and lifelong? Why has time a grudge against us? It is, unfortunately, because we have ever neglected our practice.

Without looking forward to tomorrow every moment, you must think only of this day and this hour. Because tomorrow is difficult and unfixed, and difficult to know, you must think of following the Way while you live today.

In fact, the tomorrow is not certain: it may come, it may not come. Those who know have even said that tomorrow never comes. What comes is always today. So do whatever you want to do this moment. Catch hold of your life source because tomorrow it may be too late. It is already late.

You must concentrate on Zen practice without wasting time, thinking that there is only this day and this hour. After that, it becomes truly easy. You must forget about the good and the bad of your nature, the strength or weakness of your power.

Just accept as you are, and enjoy and relish and sing and dance as you are. Acceptance is a gratitude towards existence. Anything that you don't accept means you are blaming existence. In all your prayers, and in all your prayer houses, what are you doing? You are asking God, just like a beggar, "Give me this, give me that." You don't trust existence, you demand. Demanding is not a quality of religious consciousness. Hence the real religion has no way of praying. It

only lives, and lives in such a way that the very life becomes a gratitude.

A haiku by Chōshū:

> *The moon in the water;*
> *Broken and broken again,*
> *Still it is there.*

It is almost unbelievable how Zen poets have said things. No other language has been able to rise to such heights. What Chōshū is saying:

The moon in the water;

Broken and broken again...because each time wind comes, a wave comes, the moon is broken in a thousand pieces. But again the lake becomes silent and all the broken pieces all over the lake start gathering again. Because it is a reflection the moon is never broken, it is only the reflection that is broken. And because the moon is never broken, it does not matter that its reflection is broken a thousand times.

All our bodies, all our minds, all our lives are nothing but reflections of the real moon...broken a thousand times. Still, in the innermost core of your being, the moon is as full and as perfect as ever.

Issa wrote:

> *The youngest nightingale that*
> *can rejoice*
> *Calls to its parents in a yellow*
> *voice.*

Now, you are not to be worried about what is said; these words are very indicative. Issa must have been in deep meditation and he heard the nightingale rejoicing and calling to its parents in a yellow voice. He is not saying anything about the nightingale, he is saying something about his silence. When you are in silence and a cuckoo from the bamboos starts singing, it deepens your silence.

And another poet:

> *Whatever we wear,*
> *We look beautiful,*
> *When moon-viewing.*

The moon certainly makes everything beautiful. On a full-moon night you see beauty spread all around, even to ordinary plants. Ordinary flowers are shining with joy. Small puddles of water are reflecting the full moon with as much depth as the greatest ocean.

So it does not matter which body you have; whether man or woman, bird or animal; whether you are poor or rich. In a silent space, just watching the moon and you are filled with tremendous beauty. That beauty arises in your innermost world. The moon simply triggers it.

Maneesha has asked:

Our Beloved Master,
Often images arise of their own accord during discourse and
the death phase of the meditation, and make whatever is happening

stronger and more vivid. Can visualization help, or because it is merely imagination, is it useless?

Maneesha, it is absolutely useless. No ripple has to be allowed. The silence has to be absolutely pure. Any visualization will be a disturbance, any thought will distract you from your being. So I am saying categorically: everything is useless while you are meditating. Meditation is taking you in a different direction, not of utility but of existence. And all your visualization will be of the world that you know, you cannot visualize something that you don't know. And you don't know your own self, your don't know the inner sky, so you cannot visualize it. And once you know it, there is no need to visualize, it is in your hands. You are no longer poor, you have become the richest person in the world—having nothing.

Meditation, perhaps, is the only alchemy that can transform a beggar into an emperor.

Before you become emperors, before you become buddhas again tonight, you must be remembering a little bit of yesterday. You know the path. Every day you have to go a little further, a little deeper.

A few laughs to make you light, to make you nonserious....

I am being blamed all over the world, in articles, that I am a nonserious man. They think they are condemning me—it is a compliment. They don't understand that, to me, seriousness is sickness. And to be nonserious, to be playful, to take everything as fun is, according to me, the only authentic religiousness.

Millicent Money-Butt is an extremely rich and an extremely frustrated woman. She is especially irritable today because it has been weeks since her husband or her chauffeur or her stable boy or *anybody* has made love to her. Deciding that she needs to move her energy, she calls her butler, James, upstairs to draw her a hot bath.

James knocks quietly and then enters her room. Millie turns to him slowly, and says, "James, please take my dress off."

"Yes, madam," says the butler, looking a bit shy.

"Now, James," says Millie, "please take my bra off."

"Er, yes, madam," says the shocked butler.

"And now, James," she says with fire in her eyes, "please take my panties off."

Then stepping up close to him, she orders, "James, next time I catch you wearing my clothes you will be fired!"

Jablonski gets married, but does not know what to do with his bride on the wedding night. So the next day he goes to ask advice from Doctor Gas-Bag.

"It is easy," says Gas-Bag, and takes Jablonski to the window. He points to two dogs screwing out in the street and says, "You do it just like that."

A week later, Jablonski comes back. "Well," asks the doctor, "how did it go?"

"Great, Doc," says Jablonski, proudly. "It was simple, no big deal at all. The only problem was getting my wife out into the street!"

Olga and Kowalski are living in an L.A. apartment, when a young couple moves in upstairs. Soon, every night, the Polacks hear the noise, "She-BOOM! She-BOOM!" coming from the floor above.

Olga is intrigued by the noise, and one day asks the young woman what it is.

"Oh, that," replies the woman. "We have had a slide installed in our bedroom. I lie at the bottom of it with my legs apart, and my husband slides down... She-BOOM!"

A few days pass and the young woman does not see the Kowalskis around. She finds out that Olga is in the hospital, so she goes to visit her.

"What happened to you?" she asks.

"It is a sad story," replies Olga. "My husband and I also had a slide installed in our bedroom, but we only got to try it once. Now I have had three operations, and they still can't find Kowalski."

Kronski is going to join the army, so he goes to visit his girlfriend, Dilda, to say goodbye.

"Oh, darling," cries Dilda. "I don't have a picture of you!"

So Kronski looks in his pockets, and all he has is a photo of himself standing naked. He cuts the picture in two, and gives her the top half.

Next he goes to visit his old grandmother to say goodbye.

"Oh, dear boy," says his granny. "You can't leave without giving me a picture of you."

Kronski does not know what to do, but remembering that his granny is half-blind, he gives her the bottom half of the picture. She looks at it with delight and says, "Just like your grandfather, God rest his soul. A nice bushy beard, and his necktie always hanging to one side."

Now...Nivedano...

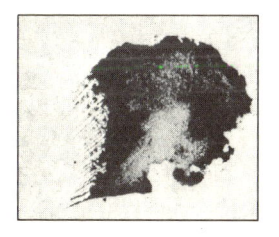

Nivedano...

LIVE ONE DAY AS A BUDDHA

Be silent,
close your eyes,
feel as if your body is frozen,
and gather all your consciousness inwards,
deeper and deeper.
At the deepest point you are the buddha.
And this buddha
has to become your whole life.
All expressions, actions,
have to arise from this center.
This center is the center of transformation.
Every seeker has been searching for it
down the ages.
This is the ancient path.
On this path
thousands have become awakened.
There is no barrier except fear—
the fear of the unknown.
Drop it.
Just rush towards it without any fear—
it is your own being.
You are not going to meet anybody else
on the way...
there is no question of fear.
This moment, this evening,
is blessed by ten thousand buddhas
who have returned home.

Nivedano...

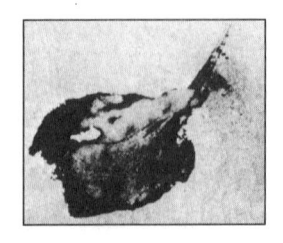

Relax... let go...
die to the body,
to the mind,
so only a throbbing consciousness
is left behind.
That is you.
That is me.
That is the very essence of existence.
Just a small taste of this silence,
a little experience of this beauty,
of this truth,
and slowly slowly your whole life
will be transformed
without your even knowing.
Your actions
will start expressing your buddhahood,
your compassion,
your love, your beauty.

Nivedano...

Call all the buddhas back to life.
Sit down for a few moments...
collecting the immense experience,
making yourself sure of it,
that you have got it.
Because you have to live it.
I am not a philosopher.
And I am not a priest.
I am a man in tremendous love

LIVE ONE DAY AS A BUDDHA

with life and existence.
All that I want to share with you
is just to make you aware
that if I can become a buddha,
there is no reason why you cannot.
We have only different bodies
but we all have the same soul.
If my soul has become aflame,
that has given me the authority to say to you
that you can also become aflame.
And this fire is eternal.
Remember it in every action,
in every expression.
Remember not to behave in any way
which will be disgraceful to a buddha.
This small discipline will bring you
to the best qualities of your being,
to their flowering.

Okay, Maneesha?
Yes, Beloved Master.

Can we celebrate ten thousand buddhas
and their evening?
Yes, Beloved Master.

SECRETLY,
A JEWEL IN HIS ROBE

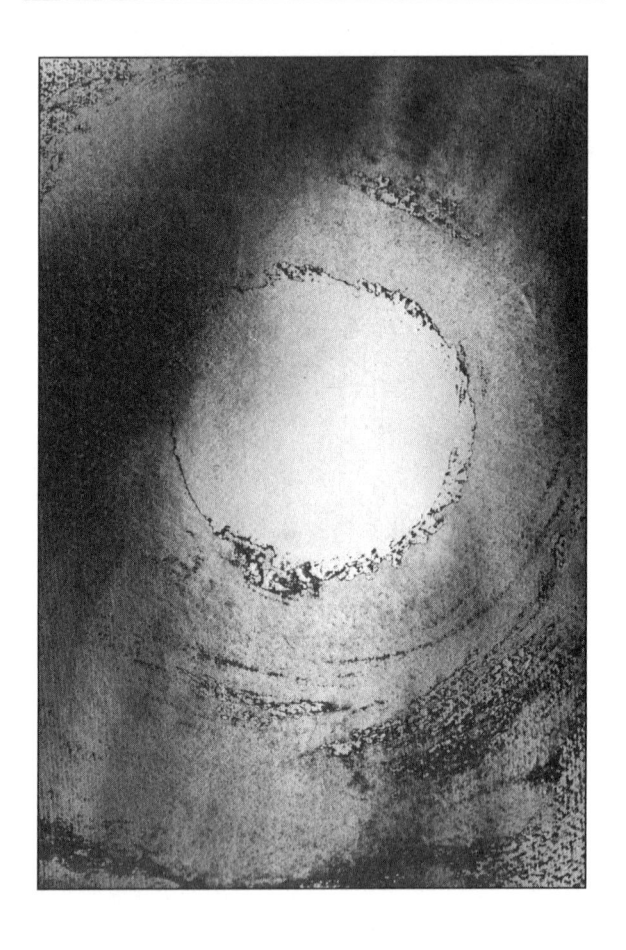

See his face
but once,
remember his name
a thousand years.

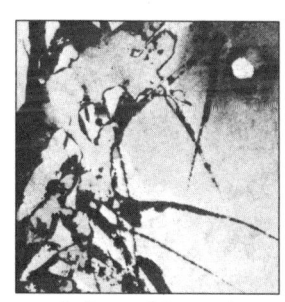

*Our Beloved Master,
Dōgen said:*
When Hsuan-Sha became enlightened he said to other monks, "The whole universe is a brilliant jewel of the Buddha-mind...."

Dōgen continued: This brilliant jewel is originally nameless, but provisionally we gave it such a name. This jewel is eternally unchangeable. Really, our body and mind, grass and trees here and there, or mountains and rivers between heaven and earth—all this is nothing but a brilliant jewel....

It is boundless from beginning to end. After all, the whole universe is one brilliant jewel, not two or three. The whole jewel is the Buddha's eye, truth itself, one phrase of truth, the light of enlightenment. At this time it never hinders the whole one, and it is round and rolls about. The function of this brilliant jewel is so clear that the sentient beings are saved by present-day avalokiteśvara or Maitreya, just by seeing their look or hearing their voice; and also the Buddhas, ancient and modern, expound the Dharma with their body.

SECRETLY, A JEWEL IN HIS ROBE

A sutra says that someone was lying drunk, when his great friend sewed a jewel in his robe, secretly. We must never fail to give this jewel to our intimate friend.

We are never drunk without being given such a jewel. Such a brilliant jewel is identical with the whole universe.

Therefore, a brilliant jewel is a brilliant jewel itself whether it rolls or not. Our realization that such is a jewel is also a jewel itself; so audible and visible is it. Therefore, it is no use wondering if we are a brilliant jewel. Whether we doubt or discern it, it is only a small, provisional viewpoint. To say more precisely: a brilliant jewel only pretends a small viewpoint.

We cannot help setting a great value on this jewel—so brilliant is the color and light of it. Who could snatch it? Who could cast it away in a market, regarding it as a tile?

We must not worry about whether we transmigrate in the six realms of existence on the law of causality. A brilliant jewel never sets aside the law of causality from beginning to end. This is the face of a brilliant jewel.

Maneesha, there is only one experience, but there can be a thousand and one expressions. Still no expression expresses it. That is its beauty, that is its immense richness, that is its infinity, eternity. No word can catch hold of it. But a man who comes home, who finds it, is also compelled by its finding to share the joy, the song, the haiku—to say something about that which cannot be said. It is an absolute compulsion. You have to do something to make the whole world aware of what you have found. Because what you have found everybody else can find, just they have forgotten the way. And it is so close that just as you close your eyes...one more step inwards and you have arrived.

All these Zen anecdotes and dialogues say the same thing again and again. But they say it very beautifully. From different standpoints, from different attitudes, they point to the same moon... hoping that perhaps, if last night you did not see it, today it may be possible from some other aspect.

The master is nothing but a great hope for the disciple, simply

waiting for you to understand a simple thing which he cannot deliver to you as matter because it is immaterial. But its pricelessness is such that he cannot ignore it either, he has to do something in order to provoke you and challenge you to search inwards. All these anecdotes are nothing but provocations, challenges. These statements have arisen out of deep love and compassion, not out of mind.

This has to be remembered about every anecdote, every dialogue, every small Zen haiku: that the master is trying in some way the impossible. And the impossible does happen once in a while. So it cannot be denied, and it cannot be said that the whole thing is futile...no need to bother about others. Enlightenment brings with itself a tremendous love for all those who are in darkness. Just because they are standing with closed eyes and they think they are blind, somebody has to nag them to open their eyes. Perhaps their eyes have been closed for so many lives. They have forgotten completely that they have eyes, so much dust has gathered.

The whole work of the master is to remove the dust and give you a challenging call so that your innermost being wakes up. And once it is awakened, you will see that all the efforts of the master were faulty; just his compassion was immense. His efforts were faulty because there is no direct way to express the inexpressible. But he still tried, knowing perfectly well that he is on an impossible journey.

When somebody awakes he can see all the faults of the master, but they don't matter. The only thing that matters is a deep gratitude to this incredible man who went on saying again and again, day after day, the same thing; hitting as hard as possible, perfectly aware that it is very rare that a man recognizes his buddhahood. But because it is only a recognition, the possibility is that everybody one day will recognize. Why not today? There is no need to postpone it.

In a way it was easier in the past. Because there were so many buddhas around, it seemed conceivable that you could also be a buddha. Unfortunately, that is not the case today. For the contemporary man, the word 'buddha' is just a word. It is very rare that you will come across a buddha in your whole life. And even if you come across him, you will not be able to recognize him because you have forgotten completely the language. You have learned the ways of

matter so much and so deeply, and they are standing as a block to your spiritual flight to the moon, to the immense sky that is your right.

Whatever the masters say, always remember: you are not to analyze the words. These are not treatises for Ph.D.'s and D. Litt.'s. These are not words spoken to spectators. Just a single spectator in this buddhafield and I can recognize immediately a hole of energy.

The day you had a poets' gathering I felt so much wounded, because I could see that you rise to your heights every day, but that day you could not rise. Just those few poets were dragging down the whole energy of the field; they were like a drainage. I was trying hard but it was impossible.

Those people will never understand that they have missed a tremendous experience because they remained spectators. They looked here, they looked there, they could not believe... They whispered to each other, "What is happening?" They could not take a jump and participate, and because of those few people the whole energy field was torn, broken.

I told Neelam that this should never happen again. I don't want a single spectator here in this field. While I am speaking, you have to be a participant, otherwise this is not the place for you. You can have your poets' gatherings and other social entertainments after I have left. But don't allow those people. It is not their fault, just they don't know what is happening here. They are curious, and their curiosity does not allow them to participate. And because they are not participating, the chain of energy that joins you all together into one whole consciousness is broken. You could not reach that day the place...the height that is becoming more and more.

Those poets tried to act as if they were participating, but it was only 'as if'. They did the gibberish, but I could see that it was just a very shallow thing for them. They were doing it because everybody else was doing it, and not to do it would look a little awkward. They sat in silence, but there was no silence. They were preparing for their poetries, thinking about what they were going to recite.

When I said to relax they looked relaxed like everybody else, but there was a qualitative difference. When you relax you know the

purpose, the meaning, the significance. They were relaxing just because everybody else was relaxing. But even relaxing, they would open their eyes and look around: What kind of relaxation...?

The whole effort is to forget the whole world. That's why I even say, "Leave the body, leave the mind," so that you can discriminate clearly what is consciousness. And this consciousness is the buddha. While you are in that consciousness you are at the highest peak of life. Just the very freedom on those heights makes one dance, sing like the birds, blossom like flowers. With no effort it happens—spontaneously. That's why after the meditation I want you always to sit for a few minutes to gather the experience, the heights, the fragrance of those depths; so that you can go on slowly remaining a buddha all the year round.

And remember, once a buddha you are always a buddha. Nobody has fallen from that point. It is just against nature.

Dōgen said:
When Hsuan-Sha became enlightened he said to other monks, "The whole universe is a brilliant jewel of the Buddha-mind."

What he is saying—what is being said by every buddha—is that the moment one becomes enlightened, he cannot see anything that is not enlightened. He sees trees standing silently in enlightenment, and the moon, brilliant in enlightenment. Your enlightenment makes you a universal consciousness—you are no more separate. It is not that you have become enlightened; for you the universe has become enlightened. And naturally, with an enlightened universe you cannot misbehave. You can only be grateful to all that exists.

Even the darkest nights don't create a complaint in you, but just a deep peace and a waiting, because soon there will be morning. The darker the night, the closer the sun. But night itself is a joy. The day has its own joys. Every moment has its own flavor. For the enlightened person, remember, it is not that he is enlightened. On the contrary, for him the whole existence has become enlightened...all light and all consciousness, all truth and all beauty.

Hsuan-Sha's statement after his enlightenment...
The whole universe is a brilliant jewel of the Buddha-mind.

Nothing is other than Buddha.

Dōgen continued: This brilliant jewel is originally nameless, but provisionally we gave it such a name.

Anything that we say about the ultimate experience is only provisional, arbitrary. So don't argue about words and don't depend on words. No word is absolutely accurate. Language simply falls far below. Those heights and those depths are beyond; words cannot reflect them. Only the great compassion of the master and his brilliance express something of the inexpressible. But that is so subtle that unless you are silent, utterly silent, you will not be able to catch hold of it.

This jewel is eternally unchangeable. Really, our body and mind, grass and trees here and there, or mountains and rivers between heaven and earth—all this is nothing but a brilliant jewel.

Everything is nothing but an expression of universal spirit. That universal spirit we call 'the buddha'. It is only a provisional name.

It is boundless from beginning to end. After all, the whole universe is one brilliant jewel, not two or three. The whole jewel is the Buddha's eye, truth itself, one phrase of truth, the light of enlightenment.

The light that radiates from the buddha is only one phase. The experience is multidimensional; it has beauty in it, it has music in it, it has truth in it—it has everything that is valuable, imperishable. Light has been chosen provisionally to express it; it is only one aspect. When we say "the enlightened one" we are just taking out one part, one aspect of the whole experience, to represent it.

At this time it never hinders the whole one, and it is round and rolls about. The function of this brilliant jewel is so clear that the sentient beings are saved by present-day avalokitesvara or Maitreya, just by seeing their look or hearing their voice; and also the Buddhas, ancient and modern, expound the Dharma with their body.

Gautam Buddha himself has said, "This very body the buddha, and this very earth the lotus paradise." Once you are enlightened your vision is so clear, and in that clarity everything shows its spirit, its life, its source. And that source is one; it is not two, it is not three.

A sutra says that someone was lying drunk, when his great friend sewed a jewel in his robe, secretly. We must never fail to give this jewel to our intimate friend.

He is just saying that this experience is impossible to give even to an intimate friend. You can provoke it but you cannot give it; it is not something in your hands. It is lying down in your intimate friend's very heart. You can make devices...just as tickling brings laughter, although there is no reasonable connection, why tickling should bring laughter.

I have known one person who does not need to be tickled. Just from far away you make the gesture, and that is enough. Here there is also one person, everybody knows her. She is sitting so buddha-like, but just if I do this right now...

(The Master jiggles his fingers in a tickling gesture towards Avirbhava. Each time He "tickles," everyone roars with laughter, and the Master Himself is chuckling behind his sunglasses. He alternates his tickling gestures with a series of hand movements to calm us down...until the next outbreak of laughter.)

And where is Anando?
(The Master, spotting Anando, begins to jiggle his hand in her direction and is laughing Himself. More waves of laughter.)

That is Anando, I could see.
This is the only way buddhahood arises: the master has to tickle.

Now do you see the effect? I have not even tickled Avirbhava, neither have I tickled Anando, and you are all laughing!
(More "tickles" and more laughter ensue.)

This tickling is called, in the sutras, *the great transmission*. I have not even touched...
(He "tickles" several people, laughing, and everyone is carried along with Him again.)

The master can only create a device. The device has no logical connection. Now do you see why you are laughing? Of course Avirbhava, at least, is tickled from far away—remote control. But why are you laughing? I have a remote control...

(The Master demonstrates his remote control on Avirbhava, and we all laugh some more. He laughs, and then motions to her to be still.)

Calm down. Just sit like a buddha...close your eyes *(He giggles)*... look inside. *(Another burst of laughter.)*

A Zen poet has written:

> *See his face*
> *but once,*
> *remember his name*
> *a thousand years.*

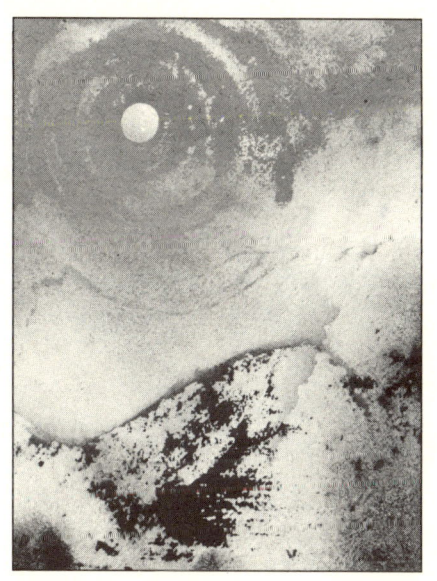

He is talking about his master. Once you have seen the face of the master, you cannot forget it for thousands of years, because in that small moment you have seen yourself. A master is, at the most, a mirror. He can show you your face if you come closer. And all discipleship is nothing but coming closer and closer and closer, so that you can see into the eyes of your master, into his gestures, your own buddhahood.

See his face
but once,
remember his name
a thousand years.

Another Zen poet:

> *One call invites*
> *one hundred comrades;*
> *one smile beckons*
> *ten thousand admirers.*

You have just seen it. Do you want to see it again?

(The Master begins to "tickle" again provoking waves of laughter, with a few chuckles from Him.) I have two remote controls—one for Avirbhava and the other for Anando. Wherever they are in the universe...just tickle and they will laugh. And with them, others will laugh for no reason at all.

I want you to understand: enlightenment is so light, so loving, so peaceful—just like a laughter. The theologians have made it so heavy, so burdensome, that people ignore it. Enlightenment should also be entertainment at the same time.

It reminds me of J. Krishnamurti's last sentence before he died, just a few months ago. He was a very serious person, and that was his only fault. He was enlightened, but he took enlightenment as a serious matter. He saw that he was enlightened and nobody else was enlightened. And he was trying hard to make people enlightened...obviously.

For seventy years—he died at the age of ninety—for seventy years, from the age of twenty, he had been working on people, and not a single person had become enlightened. You can understand his sense of deep failure and his sadness...becoming more and more serious, almost a sickness.

And the reason is clear from his last statement, "People don't take enlightenment seriously, they think it is entertainment." And that is where I differ. Enlightenment cannot be anything else other than entertainment...universal entertainment, a laughter that knows no bounds, no limits. You laugh, and the trees laugh, and the cuckoos laugh, and the clouds laugh, and the stars laugh, and the laughter goes on spreading because everybody is triggering everybody else. You need not actually trigger, just your laughter will be enough for somebody else to start laughing.

I love J. Krishnamurti, and I love his hard effort of seventy years continuously, but I am absolutely against his attitude. He was making it a serious affair. That was the fault of all the old prophets. That's why you will not find a statue of Mahavira laughing. What a miserable world, you don't allow even Mahavira to laugh. You will not find a statue of Gautam Buddha laughing. Even if Gautam Buddha laughed, people would not believe their eyes or ears: "What is happening? Such a serious man..."

But you don't understand that when the mind is gone you are just like a small child. Laughter will arise without any effort on your part. At least I am a break from the whole past, and in the future I want my people to be laughing buddhas. Serious ones we have seen enough of, they have not been able to transform humanity. Let us try another direction—of nonseriousness.

One call invites one hundred comrades.... One buddha—just his presence—magnetically pulls a thousand buddhas, ten thousand buddhas. It is a question of how great your enlightenment is, how great your compassion and love is, and how nonseriously you have taken it. Nobody likes a serious person.

Have you ever thought about it, that all the saints are serious? It is perfectly good to go and touch their feet...and be finished. Nobody wants their company. These people will be going to heaven—remember it. Heaven is overcrowded with saints. If you want the right kind of people go to the other place, where you will find poets, and you will find painters, and you will find dancers and musicians.

I am going particularly to the other place. So remember, whoever is with me will have a great journey and a meeting with great people. No saint has been of any value—no creativity, no poetry, no painting. All these people who were creators, who have made this world a little beautiful, a little more livable, are gathered in the other place.

Friedrich Nietzsche said God is dead, but he did not say why he is dead. He has to be dead, surrounded by all these idiots, eternally stinking...because most of them don't take a bath, don't wash their mouths. Laughter is absolutely unknown in paradise, poor God could not survive.

So I warn you, beware! If by chance you reach to the gates of

heaven—refuse. Don't enter in. Ask for the way to the other place. I will be waiting there for you. Ask for me and that will do.

> *Cry*
> *after cry*
> *after cry of joy—*
> *not minding*
> *the hair*
> *turning white*

This Zen poet is saying that even crying is so beautiful, so lightening, so unburdening.

Cry
after cry
after cry of joy—
not minding
the hair
turning white

Don't be worried about time…space…age. Just learn to laugh and cry totally, because these are the simplest ways to reach your innermost being.

Maneesha has asked:

Our Beloved Master,
Our most brilliant and precious jewel,
Whenever I have asked about Your beauty, You have insisted that it is the eyes of love that project beauty on You. But You do not have our experience of sitting in front of You, following—as we do—Your every movement, tracing every beloved curve and line and valley in Your face.
I know of no one else—however much I love them—that I could gaze on for years, never feeling bored, never feeling I have fathomed their beauty.

Maneesha, in that case I accept that I am unfortunate. You are blessed to have a master who is not a burden on you. You are blessed

to have a master who is not a masochist, a sadist.

I was not so blessed. I had never come across a single man whom I could have called my master. I had to work my way alone, on my own, going this way and that; falling and getting up again, nobody to guide me, nobody to give me any instruction, nobody even to indicate a finger to the moon. But it seems, just by chance, I happened to stumble upon the right place.

I am a master who had no master. So I cannot see and cannot say what you see in my eyes, in my face. But whatever you are seeing is really a pure reflection of your love and your trust. This body will wither away, but I have another body, of light. Before this body withers away, you have to become acquainted with my light body, with my inner center. And your center and my inner center are not two. In that area there is always one—neither two nor three.

Now, before we enter into our daily meditation...just to drop all burdens, all the worries of the world, and have a few good laughs. I have not found anything better to create a right space to enter into yourself, because your mind cannot understand laughter. Laughter is very illogical. A logical person cannot laugh, a logical person is confined to a very small area.

I have not heard that Kant ever laughed. He could not, he was too serious a person. Just now I was talking to you about J. Krishnamurti.... He used to come to India at least once or twice a year. He went to only three places: Varanasi, New Delhi and Bombay. I had instructed all my sannyasins, "Wherever he is, either in India or outside India, just sit in the front line wherever he is speaking. And don't forget the orange and the mala."

And that was enough. Then he would not speak on any other subject. That was enough to make him so angry, "I have been telling my whole life...!" And my people enjoyed it, they loved it. Even a few people who were not sannyasins used to go in orange, borrowing a mala from a friend.

Just a single sannyasin was enough. Then he would forget everything that he was going to say. Then he just had to condemn me, condemn sannyas, condemn everything—not understanding a simple

SECRETLY, A JEWEL IN HIS ROBE

thing, that he was being easily distracted. What does it matter? Somebody is wearing orange and having a mala...it is none of his business.

But he was a serious man. He would hit his own head. He would become so angry...particularly in Bombay, because I was in Bombay. So hundreds of sannyasins would be sitting in the front, and he would hit his head. I am so lazy that I cannot even hit my own head, let alone anybody else's. I am keeping for that purpose Zen Master Sekitō—Stonehead.

(The Master addresses Niskriya.) Where is your staff?

(Niskriya picks up his staff and shows it to the Master)

Yes, that's good, because any moment it may be needed. And I have chosen a German Zen master...because Japanese Zen masters will hit, but their hit will be just like a peacock feather. A real hit only a German knows.

And just look at his stonehead. Have you shaved your hairs or not? Shave them completely. *(Niskriya raises his eyebrows in a question, pointing to his new beard—this too?)* Yes, let it go.

Proper Sagar has arrived. Many of you may not know him—he is a very ancient sannyasin—but most of the old sannyasins will remember Proper Sagar. He is so proper in everything.

Proper Sagar goes to visit Doctor Azima. He hangs up his umbrella and his hat. Then he takes off his jacket, his shirt and tie, and his trousers—folding them up very neatly and putting them on the chair. Then he takes off his shoes and puts them under the chair, straight. Then he takes off his underwear, folds them nicely, and also puts them on the chair.

Standing stiffly in front of Azima, Sagar calmly says, "As you can see, Doctor, my left testicle hangs lower than my right one."

"Oh," smiles Azima, "but that-a is perfectly normal. You have-a nothing to worry about."

"I am not worrying," replies Proper Sagar. "But don't you think it is a bit untidy?"

Pope the Polack is on a pilgrimage in Calcutta where he makes an official visit to Mother Teresa's orphanage.

Mother Teresa is showing him around, and the Polack is bending and kissing everything in sight. Suddenly, as he bends over to kiss Mother Teresa's pride and joy, the new church organ, the pope recoils in terror. There, stretched out across the top of the organ, is a big black condom.

Purple with rage, Pope the Polack demands an explanation from Mother Teresa.

"Well," says Mother Teresa, "one of my orphans found it in a package on the street, and when I read the label it said: 'Place on organ and feel secure.'"

Harold, Bill and Gabby, three tired and hungry cowboys, are sitting around a campfire about to eat dinner. José, the cook, a grimy, stubble-faced huge Mexican guy, throws down the pot and holds up his gun.

"The first one of you jerks who makes a fuss about your supper gets trouble from me!" says José.

There is careful silence as the purple and green slop is served up, and the eating begins.

"God!" shrieks Harold, gagging and turning blue. "This stuff tastes like shit."

Then, immediately eyeing the big Mexican, Harold adds enthusiastically, "But good shit, *real* good shit."

Doctor Feelgood is visiting the insane asylum to see the latest condition of some of his patients. He is led into the first room, opens the door, and meets Charlie Rosenkrantz. At that moment Mr. Rosenkrantz is swinging an imaginary golf club in the air.

"Well, Charlie," says Feelgood. "When do you think you will be getting out?"

"No problem," replies Charlie, swinging away. "Just as soon as I hit a hole-in-one."

Feelgood shakes his head and goes on to the next room. There he finds Chester Cheese swinging an imaginary baseball bat.

SECRETLY, A JEWEL IN HIS ROBE

"Hello, Chester," says Feelgood. "And when do you think you will be getting out?"

"Oh, soon," replies Chester. "Just as soon as I hit this home-run."

Feelgood shakes his head again, and is led to the next room. He walks in and finds Donald Dickstein rubbing a bag of peanuts up against his open zipper.

"Hello, Donald," says Feelgood. "And when do you think you will be getting out?"

"Out? Are you kidding?" says Donald excitedly. "I'm fucking nuts!"

Now, Nivedano...give the beat.

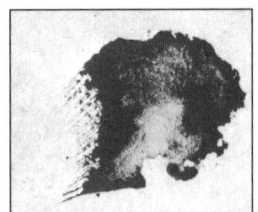 

Nivedano...

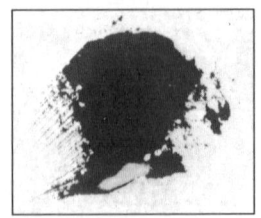 

DŌGEN

Be silent...close your eyes...
feel frozen. Collect your life energy,
your consciousness, within.
This is the place
where you have roots in the universe.
This is the place
which makes one a buddha.
Go deeper, without any fear.
It is unknown, unfamiliar,
but don't be worried—
it is your own self.

Remember these heights...
remember these depths...
remember you are part of this universe.
Drop all separation.
Just slip like a dewdrop
from the lotus leaf into the ocean.
To disappear in this ocean
is to become the ocean.

To make it more clear, Nivedano...

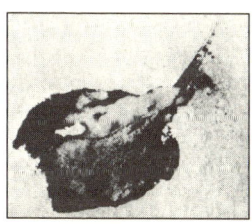 

Relax...let go...
The body is there, lying...
it is not you.
The mind is there,
maybe a few clouds still hovering around...
but it is not you.

You are the watcher on the hills.
This silent night,
and ten thousand buddhas
watching silently.
There cannot be anything greater,
or more significant.
The clouds have also joined,
the bamboos are making commentaries.

I hope there will be a day
when the whole humanity
will understand this buddhahood.
Spread this experience
to all those who are groping in darkness.

But never be a missionary;
just be a message…
loving, compassionate.
Let your whole body, your actions,
make them aware
that something immensely valuable
has happened within you;
that you are carrying a flame,
that you are carrying a fragrance,
that your eyes have become as blue
and as vast
and as deep
as the sky itself.

This I call "to be a message."
Except becoming a buddha,
there is no way
to convey what you are experiencing.
And remember:
once a buddha,
forever a buddha.

DŌGEN

Nivedano...

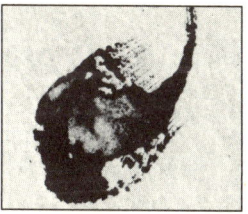 

Call all the buddhas back.
Slowly and silently...
sit for a few moments...
just reflecting...
collecting...
remembering what has happened to you...
where you have been.
Remember the route so you can go,
anytime you want,
into the temple.
You are the temple,
and deep inside you is the buddha.

Okay, Maneesha?
Yes, Beloved Master.

Can we celebrate the ten thousand buddhas?
Yes, Beloved Master.

Osho Rajneesh was born in Kuchwada, Madhya Pradesh, India, on December 11, 1931. From his earliest childhood, his was a rebellious and independent spirit, challenging all accepted religious, social and political traditions and insisting on experiencing the truth for himself rather than acquiring knowledge and beliefs given by others.

At the age of twenty-one, on March 21, 1953, Rajneesh became enlightened. He says about himself, "I am no longer seeking, searching for anything. Existence has opened all its doors to me, I cannot even say that I belong to existence, because I am just a part of it... When a flower blossoms, I blossom with it. When the sun rises, I rise with it. The ego in me, which keeps people separate, is no longer there. My body is part of nature, my being is part of the whole. I am not a separate entity."

ABOUT THE AUTHOR

He graduated from the University of Sagar with First Class Honors in philosophy. While a student he was All-India Debating Champion and the Gold Medal winner. After a nine-year stint as professor of philosophy at the University of Jabalpur, he left to travel around the country giving talks, challenging orthodox religious leaders in public debate, upsetting traditional beliefs, and shocking the status quo.

In the course of his work, Rajneesh has spoken on virtually every aspect of the development of human consciousness. From Sigmund Freud to Chuang Tzu, from George Gurdjieff to Gautam Buddha, from Jesus Christ to Rabindranath Tagore... He has distilled from each the essence of what is significant to the spiritual quest of contemporary man, based not on intellectual understanding but tested against his own existential experience.

He belongs to no tradition—"I am the beginning of a totally new religious consciousness," he says. "Please don't connect me with the past—it is not even worth remembering."

His talks to disciples and seekers from all over the world have been published in more than six hundred fifty volumes, and translated into over thirty languages. And he says, "My message is not a doctrine, not a philosophy. My message is a certain alchemy, a science of transformation, so only those who are willing to die as they are and be born again into something so new that they cannot even imagine it right now...only those few courageous people will be ready to listen, because listening is going to be risky. Listening, you have taken the first step towards being reborn. So it is not a philosophy that you can just make an overcoat of and go bragging about. It is not a doctrine where you can find consolation

ABOUT THE AUTHOR

for harassing questions... No, my message is not some verbal communication. It is far more risky. It is nothing less than death and rebirth."

Osho Rajneesh is now residing at Rajneeshdham in Poona, India, where thousands of disciples and seekers gather throughout the year to participate in the meditations and other programs offered there.

Worldwide Distribution Centers for the Works of Osho Rajneesh

Books by Osho Rajneesh are available in many languages throughout the world. His discourses have been recorded live on audiotape and videotape. There are many recordings of Rajneesh meditation music and celebration music played in His presence, as well as beautiful photographs of Osho Rajneesh. For further information contact one of the distribution centers below:

EUROPE

Belgium
Indu
Rajneesh Meditation Center
Coebergerstr. 40
2018 Antwerpen
Tel.   3/237 2037
Fax   3/216 9871

Denmark
Anwar Distribution
Carl Johansgade 8, 5
2100 Copenhagen
Tel.   01/420 218
Fax   01/147 348

Finland
Unio Mystica Shop
for Meditative Books & Tapes
Albertinkatu 10
P.O. Box 186
00121 Helsinki
Tel.   3580/665 811

Italy
Rajneesh Services Corporation
Via XX Settembre 12
28041 Arona (NO)
Tel.   02/839 2194 (Milan office)
Fax   02/832 3683

Netherlands
De Stad Rajneesh
Cornelis Troostplein 23
1072 JJ Amsterdam
Tel.   020/5732 130
Fax   020/5732 132

Norway
Devananda
Rajneesh Meditation Center
P.O. Box 177 Vinderen
0319 Oslo 3
Tel.   02/491 590

Spain
Distribuciones "El Rebelde"
Estellencs
07192 Mallorca - Baleares
Tel.   71/410 470
Fax   71/719 027

Sweden
Madhur
Rajneesh Meditation Center
Nidalvsgrand 15
12161 Johanneshov / Stockholm
Tel.   08/394 996
Fax   08/184 972

Switzerland
Mingus
Rajneesh Meditation Center
Asylstrasse 11
8032 Zurich
Tel.   01/2522 012

United Kingdom

OSHO PURNIMA DISTRIBUTION
"GREENWISE"
VANGE PARK RD., BASILDON
ESSEX SS16 5LA
Tel: 01268 584141 Fax: 01268 559919
e-mail: oshopurnima@compuserve.com
website: www.osho.co.uk

West Germany
The Rebel
Publishing House GmbH*
Venloer Strasse 5-7
5000 Cologne 1
Tel.   0221/574 0742
Fax   0221/574 0749
Telex 888 1366 rjtrd

* All books available
  AT COST PRICE

Rajneesh Verlag GmbH
Venloer Strasse 5-7
5000 Cologne 1
Tel.   0221/574 0743
Fax   0221/574 0749

Tao Institut
Klenzestrasse 41
8000 Munich 5
Tel.   089/201 6657
Fax   089/201 3056

AMERICA

United States
Chidvilas
P.O. Box 17550
Boulder, CO 80308
Tel.   303/665 6611
Fax   303/665 6612

Ansu Publishing Co., Inc.
19023 SW Eastside Rd
Lake Oswego, OR 97034
Tel   503/638 5240
Fax   503/638 5101

Nartano
P.O. Box 51171
Levittown,
Puerto Rico 00950-1171
Tel. 809/795 8829

Also available in bookstores
nationwide at Walden Books

Canada
Publications Rajneesh
P.O. Box 331
Outremont H2V 4N1
Tel.   514/276 2680

AUSTRALIA
Rajneesh Meditation & Healing Centre
P.O. Box 1097
160 High Street
Fremantle, WA 6160
Tel.   09/430 4047
Fax   09/384 8557

ASIA

India
Sadhana Foundation*
17 Koregaon Park
Poona 411 001, MS
Tel.   0212/660 963
Fax   0212/664 181

* All books available
  AT COST PRICE

Japan
Eer Rajneesh
Neo-Sannyas Commune
Mimura Building 6-21-34
Kikuna, Kohoku-ku
Yokohama, 222
Tel.   045/434 1981
Fax   045/434 5565

Books by Osho Rajneesh

ENGLISH LANGUAGE EDITIONS
RAJNEESH PUBLISHERS

Early Discourses and Writings
A Cup of Tea *Letters to Disciples*
From Sex to Superconsciousness
I Am the Gate
The Long and the Short and the All
The Silent Explosion

Meditation
And Now, and Here (Volumes 1&2)
The Book of the Secrets (Volumes 1–5) *Vigyana Bhairava Tantra*
Dimensions Beyond the Known
In Search of the Miraculous (Volume 1)
Meditation: The First and Last Freedom
Meditation: The Art of Ecstasy
The Orange Book *The Meditation Techniques of Bhagwan Shree Rajneesh*
The Perfect Way
The Psychology of the Esoteric

Buddha and Buddhist Masters
The Book of the Books (Volumes 1–4) *The Dhammapada*
The Diamond Sutra *The Vajrachchedika Prajnaparamita Sutra*
The Discipline of Transcendence (Volumes 1–4)
 On the Sutra of 42 Chapters
The Heart Sutra *The Prajnaparamita Hridayam Sutra*
The Book of Wisdom (Vols. 1&2) *Atisha's Seven Points of Mind Training*

Indian Mystics:
The Bauls
The Beloved (Volumes 1&2)

Kabir
The Divine Melody
Ecstasy – The Forgotten Language
The Fish in the Sea is Not Thirsty
The Guest
The Path of Love
The Revolution

Krishna
Krishna: The Man and His Philosophy

Jesus and Christian Mystics
Come Follow Me (Volumes 1–4) *The Sayings of Jesus*
I Say Unto You (Volumes 1&2) *The Sayings of Jesus*
The Mustard Seed *The Gospel of Thomas*
Theologia Mystica *The Treatise of St. Dionysius*

Jewish Mystics
The Art of Dying
The True Sage

Sufism
Just Like That
Mojud, The Man with the Inexplicable Life *Excerpts from The Wisdom of the Sands*
The Perfect Master (Volumes 1&2)
The Secret
Sufis: The People of the Path (Volumes 1&2)
Unio Mystica (Volumes 1&2) *The Hadiqa of Hakim Sanai*
Until You Die
The Wisdom of the Sands (Volumes 1&2)

Tantra
Tantra, Spirituality and Sex *Excerpts from The Book of the Secrets*
Tantra: The Supreme Understanding *Tilopa's Song of Mahamudra*
The Tantra Vision (Volumes 1&2) *The Royal Song of Saraha*

Tao
The Empty Boat *The Stories of Chuang Tzu*
The Secret of Secrets (Volumes 1&2) *The Secret of the Golden Flower*
Tao: The Golden Gate (Volumes 1&2)
Tao: The Pathless Path (Volumes 1&2) *The Stories of Lieh Tzu*
Tao: The Three Treasures (Volumes 1–4) *The Tao Te Ching of Lao Tzu*
When the Shoe Fits *The Stories of Chuang Tzu*

The Upanishads
I Am That *Isa Upanishad*
Philosophia Ultima *Mandukya Upanishad*
The Supreme Doctrine *Kenopanishad*
That Art Thou *Sarvasar Upanishad, Kaivalya Upanishad, Adhyatma Upanishad*
The Ultimate Alchemy (Volumes 1&2) *Atma Pooja Upanishad*
Vedanta: Seven Steps to Samadhi *Akshya Upanishad*

Western Mystics
Guida Spirituale *On the Desiderata*
The Hidden Harmony *The Fragments of Heraclitus*
The Messiah (Volumes 1&2) *Commentaries on Kahlil Gibran's The Prophet*
The New Alchemy: To Turn You On *Mabel Collins' Light on the Path*
Philosophia Perennis (Vols. 1&2) *The Golden Verses of Pythagoras*
Zarathustra: A God That Can Dance
   Commentaries on Friedrich Nietzsche's Thus Spoke Zarathustra

Zarathustra: The Laughing Prophet
  Commentaries on Friedrich Nietzsche's Thus Spoke Zarathustra

Yoga
Yoga: The Alpha and the Omega (Volumes 1–10) *The Yoga Sutras of Patanjali*
Yoga: The Science of the Soul (Volumes 1–3)
  Original title Yoga: The Alpha and the Omega (Volumes 1–3)

Zen and Zen Masters:
Poona 1974-1981
Ah, This!
Ancient Music in the Pines
And the Flowers Showered
Dang Dang Doko Dang
The First Principle
The Grass Grows By Itself
Hsin Hsin Ming: The Book of Nothing *Discourses on the Faith-Mind of Sosan*
Nirvana: The Last Nightmare
No Water, No Moon
Returning to the Source
Roots and Wings
The Search *The Ten Bulls of Zen*
A Sudden Clash of Thunder
The Sun Rises in the Evening
Take it Easy (Volumes 1&2) *Poems of Ikkyu*
This Very Body the Buddha *Hakuin's Song of Meditation*
Walking in Zen, Sitting in Zen
The White Lotus *The Sayings of Bodhidharma*
Zen: The Path of Paradox (Volumes 1–3)
Zen: The Special Transmission

The Mystery School 1986-present
Bodhidharma The Greatest Zen Master
  Commentaries on the Teachings of the Messenger of Zen from India to China
The Great Zen Master Ta Hui
  Reflections on the Transformation of an Intellectual to Enlightenment
THE WORLD OF ZEN *A boxed set of 5 volumes, containing:* *
    Live Zen
    This. This. A Thousand Times This.
    Zen: The Quantum Leap from Mind to No-Mind
    Zen: The Solitary Bird, Cuckoo of the Forest
    Zen: The Diamond Thunderbolt
ZEN: ALL THE COLORS OF THE RAINBOW *A boxed set of 5 volumes, containing:* *
    The Miracle
    Turning In
    The Original Man
    The Language of Existence
    The Buddha: The Emptiness of the Heart

OSHO RAJNEESH: THE PRESENT DAY AWAKENED ONE SPEAKS ON THE ANCIENT MASTERS OF ZEN A boxed set of 7 volumes, containing: *
Dōgen, the Zen Master: A Search and a Fulfillment
Ma Tzu: The Empty Mirror
Hyakujō: The Everest of Zen, with Bashō's Haikus
Nansen: The Point of Departure
Jōshū: The Lion's Roar
Rinzai: Master of the Irrational
Isan: No Footprints in the Blue Sky
*Each volume is also available individually

Responses to Questions:
Poona 1974-1981
Be Still and Know
The Goose is Out!
My Way: The Way of the White Clouds
Walk Without Feet, Fly Without Wings and Think Without Mind
The Wild Geese and the Water
Zen: Zest, Zip, Zap and Zing

Rajneeshpuram
From Darkness to Light Answers to the Seekers of the Path
From the False to the Truth Answers to the Seekers of the Path
The Rajneesh Bible (Volumes 1-4)

The World Tour
Light on the Path Talks in the Himalayas
The Sword and the Lotus Talks in the Himalayas
Socrates Poisoned Again After 25 Centuries Talks in Greece
Beyond Psychology Talks in Uruguay
The Path of the Mystic Talks in Uruguay
The Transmission of the Lamp Talks in Uruguay

The Mystery School 1986 – present
Beyond Enlightenment
The Golden Future
The Great Pilgrimage: From Here to Here
The Hidden Splendor
The Invitation
The New Dawn
The Rajneesh Upanishad
The Razor's Edge
The Rebellious Spirit
Sermons in Stones
YAA-HOO! The Mystic Rose
THE MANTRA SERIES:
  Satyam-Shivam-Sundram Truth-Goodness-Beauty
  Sat-Chit-Anand Truth-Consciousness-Bliss
  Om Mani Padme Hum The Sound of Silence: The Diamond in the Lotus

Hari Om Tat Sat *The Divine Sound: That is the Truth*
Om Shantih Shantih Shantih *The Soundless Sound: Peace, Peace, Peace*

Personal Glimpses
Books I Have Loved
Glimpses of a Golden Childhood
Notes of a Madman

Interviews with the World Press
The Last Testament (Volume 1)

Compilations
Beyond the Frontiers of the Mind
Bhagwan Shree Rajneesh On Basic Human Rights
The Book *An Introduction to theTeachings of Bhagwan Shree Rajneesh*
 Series I from A - H
 Series II from I - Q
 Series III from R - Z
Death: The Greatest Fiction
Gold Nuggets
The Greatest Challenge: The Golden Future
I Teach Religiousness Not Religion
Jesus Crucified Again, This Time in Ronald Reagan's America
Life, Love, Laughter
The New Man: The Only Hope for the Future
A New Vision of Women's Liberation
Priests and Politicians: The Mafia of the Soul
The Rebel: The Very Salt of the Earth
Sex: Quotations from Bhagwan Shree Rajneesh
Words from a Man of No Words

Photobiographies
Shree Rajneesh: A Man of Many Climates, Seasons and Rainbows
 Through the Eye of the Camera
The Sound of Running Water *Bhagwan Shree Rajneesh and His Work 1974-1978*
This Very Place The Lotus Paradise
 Bhagwan Shree Rajneesh and His Work 1978-1984

Books about Osho Rajneesh
Bhagwan Shree Rajneesh: The Most Dangerous Man
 Since Jesus Christ *(by Sue Appleton, LL.B.)*
Bhagwan: The Buddha For The Future *(by Juliet Forman, S.R.N., S.C.M., R.M.N.)*
Bhagwan: The Most Godless Yet The Most Godly Man
 (by Dr. George Meredith, M.D. M.B., B.S., M.R.C.P.)
Bhagwan: Twelve Days that Shook the World
 (by Juliet Forman, S.R.N., S.C.M., R.M.N.)
Was Bhagwan Shree Rajneesh Poisoned by Ronald Reagan's America?
 (by Sue Appleton, LL.B.)

ENGLISH LANGUAGE EDITIONS

OTHER PUBLISHERS

UNITED KINGDOM
The Art of Dying (Sheldon Press)
The Book of the Secrets (Volume 1, Thames & Hudson)
Dimensions Beyond the Known (Sheldon Press)
The Hidden Harmony (Sheldon Press)
Meditation: The Art of Ecstasy (Sheldon Press)
The Mustard Seed (Sheldon Press)
Neither This Nor That (Sheldon Press)
No Water, No Moon (Sheldon Press)
Roots and Wings (Routledge & Kegan Paul)
Straight to Freedom (Original title: Until You Die, Sheldon Press)
The Supreme Understanding
   (Original title: Tantra: The Supreme Understanding, Sheldon Press)
The Supreme Doctrine (Routledge & Kegan Paul)
Tao: The Three Treasures (Volume 1, Wildwood House)

Books about Osho Rajneesh
The Way of the Heart: the Rajneesh Movement
   by Judith Thompson and Paul Heelas, Department of Religious Studies,
   University of Lancaster (Aquarian Press)

UNITED STATES OF AMERICA
And the Flowers Showered (De Vorss)
The Book of the Secrets (Volumes 1–3, Harper & Row)
Dimensions Beyond the Known (Wisdom Garden Books)
The Grass Grows By Itself (De Vorss)
The Great Challenge (Grove Press)
Hammer on the Rock (Grove Press)
I Am the Gate (Harper & Row)
Journey Toward the Heart
   (Original title: Until You Die, Harper & Row)
Meditation: The Art of Ecstasy
   (Original title: Dynamics of Meditation, Harper & Row)
The Mustard Seed (Harper & Row)
My Way: The Way of the White Clouds (Grove Press)
Nirvana: The Last Nightmare (Wisdom Garden Books)
Only One Sky
   (Original title: Tantra: The Supreme Understanding, Dutton)
The Psychology of the Esoteric (Harper & Row)
Roots and Wings (Routledge & Kegan Paul)
The Supreme Doctrine (Routledge & Kegan Paul)
When the Shoe Fits (De Vorss)
Words Like Fire (Original title: Come Follow Me, Volume 1, Harper & Row)

Books about Osho Rajneesh
The Awakened One: The Life and Work of Bhagwan Shree Rajneesh
  by Vasant Joshi (Harper & Row)
Dying for Enlightenment by Bernard Gunther (Harper & Row)
Rajneeshpuram and the Abuse of Power by Ted Shay, Ph.D. (Scout Creek Press)
Rajneeshpuram, the Unwelcome Society by Kirk Braun (Scout Creek Press)
The Rajneesh Story: The Bhagwan's Garden
  by Dell Murphy (Linwood Press, Oregon)

FOREIGN LANGUAGE EDITIONS

Books by Osho Rajneesh have been translated and published in the following languages:

Chinese	German	Japanese	Punjabi	Tamil
Czech	Greek	Korean	Russian	Telugu
Danish	Gujrati	Marathi	Serbo-Croat	Urdu
Dutch	Hebrew	Nepali	Sindhi	
Finnish	Hindi	Polish	Spanish	
French	Italian	Portuguese	Swedish	

Rajneesh Meditation Centers Ashrams and Communes

There are many Rajneesh Meditation Centers throughout the world which can be contacted for information about the teachings of Osho Rajneesh and which have His books available as well as audio and video tapes of His discourses. Centers exist in practically every country.

For further information about Osho Rajneesh

Rajneeshdham Neo-Sannyas Commune
17 Koregaon Park
Poona 411 001, MS
India